John Henry Bernard

From Faith to Faith

Sermons Preached for the Most Part Before the University of Dublin

John Henry Bernard

From Faith to Faith

Sermons Preached for the Most Part Before the University of Dublin

ISBN/EAN: 9783337259006

Printed in Europe, USA, Canada, Australia, Japan

Cover: Foto ©Lupo / pixelio.de

More available books at **www.hansebooks.com**

FROM FAITH TO FAITH.

FROM FAITH TO FAITH

SERMONS

PREACHED FOR THE MOST PART BEFORE THE UNIVERSITY OF DUBLIN

BY

J. H. BERNARD D.D.

FELLOW OF TRINITY COLLEGE DUBLIN AND ARCHBISHOP KING'S LECTURER IN DIVINITY

LONDON
ISBISTER AND COMPANY LIMITED
15 & 16 TAVISTOCK STREET COVENT GARDEN
1895

LONDON:
PRINTED BY J. S. VIRTUE AND CO., LIMITED
CITY ROAD.

COLLEGIO

SANCTAE ET INDIVIDVAE TRINITATIS

PIETATIS CAVSA.

"*For I am not ashamed of the Gospel of Christ: for it is the power of God unto salvation to every one that believeth; to the Jew first, and also to the Greek. For therein is the righteousness of God revealed from faith to faith: as it is written, The just shall live by faith.*"—ROMANS i. 16, 17.

CONTENTS.

                                                                                     PAGE

1. THE KNOWLEDGE OF GOD (1 *Cor*. xiii. 9) 7
    Preached before the University of Oxford, Septuagesima, 1895.

2. NICODEMUS (*St. John* iii. 6) 33
    Preached before the University of Dublin, Trinity Sunday, 1894.

3. EVOLUTION AND THE DOCTRINE OF THE INCARNATION
    (1 *Cor*. xv. 45) 47
    Preached before the University of Dublin, Second Sunday in Lent, 1893.

4. CHRIST THE TRUTH (*St. John* xiv. 6) 63
    Preached before the University of Oxford, Twenty-second Sunday after Trinity, 1894.

5. THE REVELATION OF LIFE IN CHRIST (*Rev*. i. 18). . 89
    Preached in St. Patrick's Cathedral, Dublin, at the Opening of the General Synod, April 10th, 1893.

6. THE EDUCATION OF THE FAITHFUL (*St. John* xiv. 26) . 103
    Preached before the University of Dublin, Sunday after Ascension Day, 1890.

7. THE TOUCHSTONE OF TRUTH (1 *Tim*. iii. 15) . . . 117
    Preached before the University of Dublin, Whitsun Day, 1890.

8. THE TEACHING OFFICE OF THE CHURCH (*Eph*. iv. 11—14) 131
    Preached before the University of Dublin, Sunday next before Advent, 1890.

CONTENTS.

9. THE LETTER AND THE SPIRIT (2 *Cor.* iii. 6) . . . 145
   Preached before the University of Oxford, Twenty-second Sunday after Trinity, 1893.

10. THE INSPIRATION OF HOLY SCRIPTURE (*Gal.* iv. 22—24) 167
    Preached before the University of Dublin, Fourth Sunday in Lent, 1891.

11. THE WORD OF GOD (i.), (*St. Mark* vii. 9--13) . . 181
    Preached before the University of Dublin, Sunday next before Advent, 1893.

12. THE WORD OF GOD (ii.), (*Psalm* cxix. 105) . . . 197
    Preached before the University of Dublin, Advent Sunday, 1893.

13. THE RESURRECTION OF THE BODY (1 *Cor.* xv. 35—38) . 213
    Preached before the University of Dublin, Second Sunday after Easter, 1892.

14. THE UNITY OF THE SPIRIT (*Eph.* iv. 3—6) . . . 229
    Preached before the University of Dublin, Whitsun Day, 1895.

15. THE ATHANASIAN CREED (*St. Mark* xvi. 16) . . . 245
    Preached before the University of Dublin, Trinity Sunday, 1895.

16. THE CHARACTER OF ST. THOMAS (*St. John* xx. 28) . 261
    Preached at an Ordination held in St. Patrick's Church, Ballymena, by the Lord Bishop of Down and Connor and Dromore, St. Thomas' Day, 1890.

17. THE GRACE OF ORDERS (*Eph.* iv. 7) 275
    Preached at an Ordination held in Christ Church Cathedral, by the Lord Archbishop of Dublin, Third Sunday after Epiphany, 1892.

THE KNOWLEDGE OF GOD.

"We know in part."—1 Cor. xiii. 9.

Preached before the University of Oxford,
Septuagesima, 1895.

THE KNOWLEDGE OF GOD.

ON Septuagesima Sunday we seem to be presented in the Lessons read at Morning Prayer with a great comparison, the comparison between the kingdom of nature and the kingdom of grace. In the First Lesson we have a simple description of those methods of the divine working by which the world has come to be what we find it. As we listen to the "psalm of Creation" contained in the opening paragraphs of the Book of Genesis, our thoughts travel back to the first movements of life upon the earth, to the origin of species, and the beginning of that struggle for existence which seems to be almost a condition of life. In the Second Lesson, on the other hand, we have depicted a new heaven and a new earth which are to endure when the first heaven and the first earth shall have passed away. In that vision of the future there is much that is in striking contrast with the vision of the past. Here man's origin, there his destiny. Here the evolution of worlds, the growth of species, progressing by slow and painful steps in accordance with natural law; there the City of God "coming down from heaven as a bride adorned for her husband," and "the tabernacle of God established with men."* Here struggle, conflict, perhaps survival, perhaps death; there neither death nor conflict nor sorrow, for "the first things are passed away."

There are few topics more familiar to the student of theology than the comparison which is thus suggested to us in the services of to-day. The analogy between nature and religion! It is the most familiar of themes. It dominates much of our speculation on religious subjects; for it is so suggestive, so full of hints for the interpreting of the revelation of God whether in nature or in history. The recorded experience of St. Paul that "the invisible things of Him from the creation of the world are clearly seen, being understood by the things that are made,"† has found glad response in the experience of not a few, who have found the most fruitful interpretation of nature to be that which views it as a sacrament of the divine working, who find their best hopes for the hidden destinies of mankind in the unfaltering

* Rev. xxi. 2. † Rom. i. 20.

providence which has guided it in the past. "What if earth," we say with Milton,

> "Be but the shadow of heaven, and things therein
> Each to the other like, more than on earth is thought?"

But the picture drawn by the Seer of the Apocalypse, though challenging comparison with the Hebrew record of creation, points, as I have said, rather to a contrast than to a comparison. Things must, indeed, be like each other, *ejusdem generis*, before they can be contrasted at all. We do not contrast the colour of the ocean with the sound of a bell. And so the very contrast which is so suggestive and so striking derives its significance from the similarities between the two pictures. The heaven and the earth of the first book of the Bible have their counterpart in the new heaven and the new earth of the last book. The heavenly City is not a city whose ways shall be altogether strange to us, for it is in a new Jerusalem that the saints shall have their everlasting rest. But though this be true, yet there is no complete analogy. We have no reason to expect natural law everywhere in the spiritual world. The analogy between what we call the natural and supernatural is real and fruitful, but it does not furnish us with anything like materials from which to construct a complete theological system. The fact which Guizot expressed by saying that "natural religion exists only in books," witnesses of itself to the felt incapacity of the human intellect to give any satisfying answer to the problems which inevitably present themselves as soon as man begins to think about himself and his relation to the Supreme. And even where the premises of the Christian revelation have been taken as a starting-point, the attempt to draw conclusions as to the nature of God or the future destiny of man has often ended in something quite inconsistent with other equally true premises which have been overlooked. Aristotle, it is an oft-quoted saying, was the first bishop of the Arians. Logic has its use, but it has also its appropriate limits of exercise, which it cannot transgress without intellectual disaster. And when Luther, in his trenchant way, said that Aristotle was "an accursed, mischief-making heathen," we may suppose that he had in his mind the danger of becoming so enthralled by the logic of the schools that we begin to regard its methods as the only possible avenues to the Palace of Truth.

In short, "the analogy of religion, natural and revealed, to the constitution and course of nature," to use the cumbrous but exact phrase of Butler, is not like a map by which we may steer our course in our excursions into a new land. A map would be very useful, for the country is at once strangely like and strangely unlike that of daily experience. What looks like a highway may be but a track leading to the wilderness; we find ourselves unable to apply our knowledge to the new conditions by which we are surrounded. Rather is the information supplied by analogical reasoning to be compared to a series of pictures of the new country drawn for us in outline by a master hand. They do not serve to guide us in our journey; but as we travel in the right path under the guidance of One wiser than ourselves, we are assured from time to time that we have not wandered into the wilderness, but are on the road to the City where we would be, by the recognition of this and that feature of the country which is familiar to us from the pictures that have been long in our possession. Analogy is not a safe guide; it is a welcome, though not an indispensable, verification. If we could always trust to its guidance our knowledge of the unseen would be of the same general character as our knowledge of the seen, subject to the same laws and acquired in the same fashion. But this it is not. "We know in part," as St. Paul reminds us in the text. And it is the grasp of this serious truth which gives to what is called Agnosticism its strength and its plausibility. Every one will agree that our knowledge of the facts and laws of the natural world is only partial, though true and valuable as far as it goes; but every reverent mind will grant as well that our knowledge of the supernatural world is even less extensive and less systematic. All life is full of surprises, the religious life most of all. The best Christian theology has ever been careful to insist on this limitation of our knowledge.

Thus Origen frankly conceded it to Celsus, when constructing his famous Defence of the Faith. And not only Origen. The Athanasian Creed itself, sometimes supposed to reach the climax of positive and confident statement, bids us remember the immensity, the immeasurableness of the Godhead. Theologians of repute have not been wanting who have gone so far as to say that the *via negationis* is the only safe road along which theology may travel. And though we are not required to agree with such a statement as this, it is at least true that any other route is full of pitfalls and snares for the unwary. Data have, indeed, been furnished by revelation; but when we try to combine these data into a consistent system, we find ourselves continually at fault. At every step we need to remember the counsel of the wise man who in the same breath that he declares that " every word of God is tried," gives us the warning, " Add thou not unto His words, lest He reprove thee, and thou be found a liar." *

But, observe, to grant all this is not to accept

* Proverbs : xx. 5, 6.

the Agnosticism which, in all ages of the world, has declared the helplessness of human effort when directed towards the knowledge of the things best worth knowing, the knowledge of those unseen things which are eternal. It is merely to recognise the fact that the analogy which we are impelled to look for between the natural and the spiritual is not complete enough to justify us in treating it as a foundation for a superstructure of theory. And once we get outside the conditions of our own personal experience, the experience of that society of persons called humanity, we can only know that which has been revealed.

What is the witness of this personal experience? Does it tell us nothing about God and the world of spirit? Is it impossible to know anything beyond the facts of sense? "We know in part"; do we know at all? To this question we must seek an answer. We need not, indeed, expect any answer which has not been given before; for men have been asking this question ever since they began to think. But it is sometimes not without profit to retrace for ourselves the path by which familiar and important conclusions have been reached by others.

First, then, it has often been urged with great force that the sense of limitation which we all experience itself supplies us with some information of the deepest moment for the conduct of life. To be conscious of limits (it is a commonplace of philosophers) is, in a sense, to have got beyond them, for it is to recognise that there is something beyond. To perceive, with Bacon, that "the subtlety of nature far surpasses the subtlety of the human mind," is to perceive that the answer to the riddles of life cannot be expressed in terms of matter and motion. *Omnia exeunt in mysterium.* Everywhere we are surrounded by unseen forces, which we cannot reduce to law. Between us and their proper home there hangs a veil, the Veil of Isis, which no man can lift; but we have learnt, at least, that beyond that veil is the secret of the world's life. Here is the sphere of religion; for it is the sense of reverence in the presence of mystery not yet revealed that is the root of all religion worthy of the name. If our Agnosticism but leads us to this, then it has done good service to our faith. It is a Christian, not an Agnostic, doxology which ascribes "honour and power eternal" to "the King of Kings who dwelleth in light unapproachable, whom no man hath seen or can see."[*]

I do not know where we shall find this thought better expressed than in a strange saying unrecorded in the New Testament, but ascribed to the Christ in early Christian literature. "He that wonders shall be king. . . . Look with wonder at that which is

[*] 1 Tim. vi. 16.

before you." This (it is the commentary of Clement) is the first step to knowledge.* "He that wonders shall be king." Reverence is a condition of insight, as insight is a condition of rule. He that does not see that there is anything worthy of wonder in the facts of life, shall never so interpret them aright, that he can place them in their true mutual relations, and thus become master of their secret. So much, indeed, is admitted by many serious and thoughtful persons who yet feel that the title "Agnostic" best describes their attitude to the unseen. And if we could get no further than this, the word would be the most appropriate that we could use. But surely this is not all that can be said. For reverence in the presence of the unknown, although it be the root of religion, yet is not the whole of religion. Reverence is a condition of knowledge, but is not to be identified with it. An apostolic writer includes knowledge among Christian graces.† The inscription "to an unknown God"‡ could not fitly be placed upon a Christian altar. Can we, then, get any farther? Can we, by any means, know God?

The apologetic literature of the eighteenth cen-

---

* Ap. Clem. Alex. Strom. ii. 9, 45. θαυμάσον τὰ παρόντα, βαθμὸν τοῦτον πρῶτον τῆς ἐπέκεινα γνώσεως ὑποθέμενος . . . . ὁ θαυμάσας βασιλεύσει καὶ ὁ βασιλεύσας ἀναπαυθήσεται.
† 2 Peter i. 6.   ‡ Acts xvii. 23.

tury answered this question in a straightforward fashion enough. It appealed to the facts of nature as revealed to observation, and to the facts of history as established by testimony; and it declared that the only explanation of the one and the other was to be found in a personal God ruling the universe and entering into relations with mankind. And I am far from desiring to suggest that, in point of logic, the defence thus offered for Theism is not sound, or that in controversy of this kind the Christian apologist does not occupy the more philosophical position. But it can hardly be denied that arguments of this character, however excellent, have for ourselves little attractive power. They serve as a confirmation of belief already accepted; they do not, as a rule, inspire belief; and they certainly do not lead to the knowledge of God in the sense in which that knowledge is "life eternal." And for this various reasons might be suggested.

It might be said that the unpopularity of books like Paley's "Evidences" is partly due to the spirit of the age, which shrinks from the idea of certainty on almost any topic. As in the days of the decay of Greek philosophy and of Greek national life, suspension of judgment is supposed to be the mental attitude most worthy of a thoughtful person. To have positive opinions is regarded as the mark of a vulgar and shallow mind. And so a book which attempts to prove anything on a subject like theology is viewed with suspicion.

But, you say, whatever be thought of Paley, Butler's famous treatise is still highly esteemed, and yet it, too, is a product of the eighteenth century. Yes, but it is worth while to observe the cause of the difference. Butler, it may be safely said, owes the honourable position he still occupies in the province of theology not only to the greatness of his mental powers and his masterly grasp of the problems under discussion, but also to the tone of uncertainty with which he so often speaks, arising out of that deep sense of reverence which we feel was characteristic of the man. He does not talk about a "trial of the witnesses," but about the ignorance of man, the difficulty of arriving at truth, the consequent need of caution, the impropriety of over-confident theological speculation. And he nowhere better shows his great superiority to his age than in his unfailing recognition of the mysteriousness of life, and the awful majesty and power and holiness of Him who is the Lord of life; in short, in that reverence in the presence of mystery of which I have spoken as the root of religion.

There is, however, another and a deeper reason, quite unconnected with the temper of the present age, for the failure of all apologetic literature to produce religious conviction, to convince men that they may—that they do—know God. The practice of regarding treatises on Christian evidences as if they were competent to generate Christian belief, has been indeed an inheritance of evil bequeathed to us from the eighteenth century. That cannot be the appropriate method of arriving at spiritual truth, which is possible only for a cultivated and industrious minority. At the end of a long life Renan declared that "there are in reality but few people who have a right not to believe in Christianity."* And this at least is seriously true, that the number of those who have weighed the historical evidence for the story of the Gospels is and must remain but small. It rarely happens (I do not say never) that those who do not believe in the story to begin with are sufficiently in earnest in their examination to take the calm and dispassionate and prolonged survey of the facts which the importance of the matter, from the point of view of a Christian, demands. Nay! we do not arrive—we are not intended to arrive—by syllogisms at a knowledge of the Supreme. "Hidden from the wise and prudent, and revealed unto babes,"† —they are the words of One wiser than the sons of

---

* *Recollections of my Youth* (Eng. Trans.), p. 125.
† St. Matt. xi. 25.

men—not because ignorance is better than wisdom, but because wisdom of the intellectual sort does not come into the question at all. If there is one characteristic more than another which the modern world, with its experience of many religions, regards as essentially belonging to true religion, it is its catholicity. It must be for all sorts and conditions of men. But if the knowledge of God were attainable only by the path of logical inference, then it would be possible only for the few, the elect, the sages of philosophy. It has been well said that "it would defeat the purpose of the revelation made to us, if the hard-headed should have an advantage in accepting it over the humble-minded."* And this is true not only of Christianity, but of religion in any proper sense of that word. The processes of the discursive understanding are not the normal and appropriate modes of reaching the knowledge of God. To suppose that they are, is to treat the acquisition of religious truth as an impossibility for the vast majority of mankind. And if religion be a reality at all, such a conclusion would be no less grotesque than appalling.

But, it may be asked, if the inferences of the logical understanding do not lead to the knowledge of God, what other means have we got for acquiring

* Bishop Temple's *Bampton Lectures*, p. 215.

it, for the evidence of the bodily senses is here out of the question? Does not such an admission really require us to rest in silent reverence for an unknown and unknowable mystery?

You will have anticipated the answer that every religious man will give. The knowledge of God is not a kind of knowledge of which we have no personal experience; it is exactly the same kind of knowledge as that which we have of a human friend. I do not desire to enter into high questions as to the nature of human personality, and the light flashed upon it by the revelation that man was made in "the image and likeness of God." It is, indeed, the less necessary, as this side of the matter has recently received full and lucid discussion, if I may be permitted to say so, in the thoughtful and striking Bampton Lectures for 1894. But the point which I wish to urge is simply this. Every science has its own appropriate and appointed methods. And thus knowledge of God cannot be declared unattainable because it is not derived either from the bodily senses or from the discursive understanding. For our knowledge of our human friends is gained in neither of these ways, and yet no one has any doubt about its reality. Like the conclusions of natural science, it can be submitted to tests—tests of observation and experiment; but it is gained in a different fashion, through fellowship, through the commerce of mind with mind, of heart with heart. In such communion the intellectual faculties do not play the chief part; for in all intercourse between persons the consciousness of self is more or less in the background. We do not say to ourselves, I am I, and this is my friend, who is different from me, whose personality is distinct from mine. But we commune with him either by words or by silent sympathy, without any analysis of what our converse means. To attempt such an analysis is at once to break the sympathetic bond. We can give a rational explanation of a past act of intercourse; but while it is present with us it is not to be reduced to a logical formula. Thus the knowledge of God is transcendental, if you will; but if so, the knowledge of human friends is transcendental also. And the greatness of the object of our affections does not change the character of the intercourse; it rather tends to repress that undue consciousness of self which is destructive of all communion between persons. Does it render human friendship impossible, that one of the two comrades is vastly inferior to the other in intellectual powers? Nay, for though he has no such store of information, no such quick and masterful intelligence as his friend, still he knows him well. He knows in part, but he knows. And so it is, it may be, for us all with the knowledge of that unseen Friend, who is about our path and about our bed, who spies out all our ways.

This, believe me, is no fine-drawn speculation, without practical issues. It is from the failure to recognise that God is a Person that many give up in despair that quest after Him which is the most serious quest in life for each of us. Here is a not uncommon case. A man is quite satisfied with the intellectual guarantees of Theism, or—let us say, to be definite—of Christianity. They seem to him, when he thinks about them, amply sufficient to justify belief, and indeed to be so great that his belief might well take rank as knowledge. But yet they do not give him what they seemed to promise. He has not reached the goal on which his eyes are fixed. The knowledge of God is not his—he cannot, he dare not, conceal it from himself. The experiences of pious persons recorded in religious biography, the experiences of his own friends half disclosed in the shy intercourse of Englishmen, are not for him. He begins to think that they require a special religious sense in which he is deficient. And so the days pass, and his intellectual satisfaction yields him no real content. A half glimpse, now and again, of the spiritual life is granted to him, but he dares not trust these moments of exaltation. He is so terribly afraid of mistaking dross for gold, that he is in danger of treating gold as if it were dross. The dry light of intellect does not reveal to him the kingdom of grace, and he will walk by no other light.* God! what is God? A philosophic abstraction, a soul of the world, a stream of tendency, a beneficent law!

" Only a cloud and a smoke who was once a pillar of fire,
The guess of a worm in the dust, and the shadow of its desire."

Vanity of vanities! He has forgotten that God is a Person. He has been seeking from a word, or at best from an abstract idea, that sympathy which can only be gained in personal intercourse, which can only be gained through love.

And here is no paradox of method peculiar to religion. It is a truism that in human intercourse all knowledge of persons is preceded by love. We do not entrust the writing of the life history of any-one for whose memory we have veneration to a stranger, no matter how competent a literary artist he may be, no matter how exact his acquaintance with the external facts of that life history. For we feel, and with a true instinct, that knowledge is hardly worthy of the name which is not quickened by sympathy and has not grown by love. "The

* "Nothing is easier," said Dr. Newman, " than to use the word God, and mean nothing by it at all."

heart has its own order," as Pascal says.* Love is the condition of knowledge; it precedes it in the order of time. Love first, knowledge afterwards: is not this what we daily experience in the case of friends, of parents, of husband, of wife, of children? We do not wait to love our friends until we have tabulated and examined the motives which rule their conduct; for it is only by the aid of love that these motives can be rightly and fully interpreted. The child does not know its mother's character before it begins to love her. If it did not love her first, it would be but a poor knowledge that it would ever gain of the wealth of loving care that is lavished upon its little life. And in the highest of all earthly relationships, is not the order the same? Men and women do not, in the first instance, weigh the character and the principles of those upon whom they are about to pour out their heart's affection. No! love which waited for such an inquiry would not be love; and the knowledge which was gained without the aid of love would be unsatisfying indeed.

So is it, and so must it be, with the knowledge of God. So it was that St. Paul prayed for the Philippian Christians, that their "love might

* "Le cœur a son ordre; l'esprit a le sien, qui est par principes et démonstrations; le cœur en a un autre. On ne prouve pas qu'on doit être aimé, en exposant d'ordre les causes de l'amour; cela serait ridicule." (Pascal, *Pensées*, ii. p. 265.)

THE KNOWLEDGE OF GOD.

abound more and more in knowledge."* The steps to this knowledge are not syllogism, syllogism, syllogism; but reverence, worship, love. Reverence, first of all, in the presence of that which is immeasurably higher and holier than our own petty and insignificant and self-centred life; so that we cry, "What is man that Thou art mindful of him, and the son of man that Thou so regardest him?"† And then, as we remember that the Almighty and All-pure is a Person, a Person in whose image we ourselves are made, our reverence passes into worship. Not at once, indeed, for this, the first step, is the most anxious, the most difficult of all. The soul that unfeignedly worships will not wait long before it knows something, little though it be, of the joys of the spiritual life, of the unfaltering love of God. And the soul that loves will know enough for its own needs, and will rest in quiet faith and hope.

But it does need a co-operation of the will to take this first step where reverence is converted into worship; it needs unceasing effort to realise the personality of the Supreme. It is so easy to be vague, so hard to be definite; and yet definite we must be. For if devotion have not dogma to fall back upon, it will in the end become hysterical and unmeaning.

* Phil. i. 9. † Ps. viii. 4.

Is it not at this point that the truth of God in Christ meets us, and enlightens that which was before obscure? For the point for most of us, where reverence passes into worship, is the point at which we take home to ourselves, never to be abandoned, the truth that God became man. It is because we do not fix our gaze upon this and upon its consequences—upon this the one answer to all the riddles of life—that we feel our worship to be vague and unreal. "Lord, show us the Father, and it sufficeth us,"* said the apostle. So we too say, "Show us the Father"; that and nothing short of it will satisfy. But the Son of Man answers now as He did then, with something of grave and pitiful rebuke, "Have I been so long time with you, and hast thou not known me?" We ask to see the full glory of the Godhead, to see God face to face, even here and now; and yet He is, though veiled, in our midst. We have not perceived Him because of that capacity for inattention to what is familiar, which is the secret of so many of our failures in the spiritual life. He is in our midst, in prayer, and in sacrament; and yet we wilfully turn aside, and say, "Show us the Father."

Oh! if we be wise, we shall not so do. We shall not demand ecstatic visions of the Supreme, while

* St. John xiv. 8.

we are yet only learners in Christ's school. We shall patiently seek Him in the familiar ordinances in which He has pledged His presence and His blessing, nothing doubting that His glory will be revealed to us at last.

"The wise men did by starlight seek the Sun,"*

and we shall not refuse to walk by the light that has been given to us, dim though at times it seem to be. So worship shall pass into love, and love into that knowledge which is itself eternal life.

* Quarles' *Emblems*.

NICODEMUS.

"That which is born of the flesh is flesh, and that which is born of the Spirit is spirit."—St. John iii. 6.

Preached before the University of Dublin,
Trinity Sunday, 1894.

NICODEMUS.

THE Gospel for Trinity Sunday seems to have been chosen with special reference to the teaching which is appropriate to this, the crowning festival of the Christian year. We have presented to us in the third chapter of St. John the difficulties of a thoughtful and well-educated man who has been brought for the first time face to face with the creed of Christ. It is not the practical claims which Christ makes upon his life that distress him, but the intellectual difficulties which His teaching presents. And this is the side of Christian doctrine which forces itself upon our attention on Trinity Sunday, when we are reminded that the explanation of that wonderful life and work of Jesus Christ which we have been following, step by step, since Christmas, is not only to be sought in the needs of human nature, but lies deep in the character and personality of the Supreme.

The story of Nicodemus is familiar. He is mentioned by no evangelist save St. John, and by him only on three occasions; and yet from these brief fragments of history we can obtain a tolerably clear idea of what manner of man he was. He was a "ruler of the Jews," a person of high ecclesiastical and civil position at Jerusalem, who had been attracted by the fame of the strange teacher, whose teaching was the spiritual novelty of the time. It might be of some value, he thought, and so he would go and make inquiries in person. But it would not be seemly that Nicodemus should be found receiving instruction from the lips of an unauthorised preacher; it would be more prudent to wait upon him in private. And so he went by night. For Nicodemus was a timid man in spite of—perhaps, in consequence of—his high position. He could not afford to compromise himself. And it is worth while to observe that this characteristic comes out every time we hear of him. When the Pharisees in disgust at the influence of Jesus would have had Him arrested and brought before them, and in indignation at the infatuation of the people, declare that "this multitude which knoweth not the law is accursed," it is Nicodemus, indeed, that ventures to say a word on behalf of the Prophet of Galilee, but it is a very cautious word. "Doth our law," he suggests, "judge a man except it first hear from himself what he doeth?"* He is careful not to commit himself, but shelters his defence of Jesus behind a general principle of law. And, like most half-hearted advocates, he does not meet with much respect, for the Pharisees would vouchsafe no other than the scornful answer, "Art thou also of Galilee? Search and see, that out of Galilee ariseth no prophet."

And, in the last scene in which Nicodemus appears in history (though legend has been busy with his name) we can trace the same spirit of caution. When Joseph of Arimathea had secured from Pilate the permission to take down from the cross the sacred body of the Crucified, Nicodemus is ready to aid him in the sorrowful task, although he has not had courage, as it seems, to approach the Roman governor in the first instance. "There came also Nicodemus," says the evangelist,† "bringing a mixture of myrrh and aloes." He is now convinced that Jesus is his rightful Master, and he will not spare time or cost to do Him honour; but yet he does not desire to run unnecessary risks. The man who assisted in that last act of loving service was indeed the same man who apologetically hinted to the Pharisees that they ought to be careful not to transgress the law in

* St. John vii. 51.   † St. John xix. 39.

their relentless hate—who when he first came to the Lord came by night.

It is not, however, so much the man's physical timidity that I wish to speak of as that intellectual timidity often found in a highly cultivated nature, which is plainly to be observed in the report of his discussion with our Lord preserved for us by St. John. A candid and honest man we need not doubt that he was; he seems to have had a genuine desire to ascertain the truth. And his questionings deserve the closer scrutiny because of their likeness to the questionings of seekers after Christ in our own time. It is not hard to see that the character of Nicodemus is a type of which we meet with examples every day. "Rabbi," he begins, "we know that Thou art a teacher sent from God, for no man can do these miracles that Thou doest except God be with him." So do we still approach Christ. We recognise that there is something noble in the message of the Gospel. We disclaim all sympathy with those who would pretend that Christianity has done the world more harm than good. The *Gesta Christi* have been, and still are, beneficent to the race. He must have been a teacher from God, for no man can effect these achievements unless God's grace prevent and follow him. But Christ cuts short our patronising approval by the uncompromising words with which He answered Nicodemus. "Except a man be born again he cannot see the kingdom of God." You are not, He seems to say, in a position to pass judgment at all. Who are you that you should judge me? The growth of the kingdom of God has an earthly side, indeed, which you may see; but you know nothing about the secret of its vitality unless you have received a spiritual impulse from the Supreme. To see that kingdom you must be born again, born from above.

It was a startling figure, though it can hardly have been absolutely new to a member of the Jewish Sanhedrim. The beginnings of spiritual life had been spoken of as a new birth in the schools of the wise in Judæa, and the figure was probably no more new to Nicodemus than it is to us. But, like some, perhaps, among us, he had never been at the pains to understand what it meant. And so his reply expresses with precision the objection with which men to-day meet the message of grace. "How can a man be born when he is old?" How can he put himself into the attitude of a person on the threshold of life? Surely we are but the victims of our breeding and our education. Inherited dispositions, acquired habits, daily companionships, all have left their mark upon us. How can we assume the position of one facing the responsibilities of life for the first time? To be born again! Ah! however much we may long to recall the innocence of childhood, that can never come back. For better or for worse, we are what we are; whether through our own fault or not does not greatly matter now. And if a man cannot see the kingdom of God unless this process of growth and education be undone, then there is little hope for us. But the Lord's answer explains to us that we have an utterly false idea of His teaching, if we suppose that it does not recognise the influence of inheritance and training and environment in the formation of character. It recognises it to the fullest extent. "What is born of the flesh is flesh." Certainly it is. Our temper and our natural dispositions are the inevitable and necessary consequence of a long series of events stretching backward from the present moment throughout our own lives and the lives of our ancestors to a past so remote that it makes one dizzy to think of it. That is all true. "What is born of the flesh is flesh." But it is also true that "what is born of the Spirit is spirit," and it is, therefore, not subject to the limitations or the laws of the flesh. "Marvel not that I said to thee, ye must be born again," repeated the Christ. Little wonder that, as natural birth is the introduction to fresh powers and fresh opportunities, so, too, the entrance upon the spiritual life should alike disclose new capacities of spiritual achievement.

And the grace which the divine Spirit gives is not to be nicely calculated and reduced to rule. For the grace of the Spirit is as the wind which bloweth where it listeth, as well in its conformity to hidden law, as in the mystery of its origin and its destiny. We hear its voice and see its effects, but cannot tell whence it comes or whither it goes. There is no calculus yet devised for measuring its force, no subtle psycho-physic which shall predict how and when it will display itself; but it is there. So is it true that "except a man be born again he cannot see the kingdom of God," for it is only by the grace of the Spirit that the life of the Spirit can be lived.

And Nicodemus, startled at the freedom and the familiarity with which spiritual gifts are spoken of, asks the question, "How can these things be?" And then the tone of the Christ seems to change from that of calm and gracious explanation to that of stern rebuke. "How can these things be? Art thou the teacher of Israel and understandest not these things?" Do you really imagine—He says it to us as well as to Nicodemus—that you can explain all the facts of human life and love by your laws of heredity and development? Do you really contend that there is no room in life for spiritual force, no possibility of its operation? Do you not believe in your own free will, in your power to refuse the evil and choose the good? Are you the teacher of Israel, and yet a man who believes in nothing but what he can see or touch? If so, you are no fit hearer of my doctrine. If when I tell you earthly things, speak to you of familiar facts of daily life, you do not believe, you are not at all likely to believe if I go on to speak of heavenly things. There is no profit in discussing the conditions of membership in the kingdom of God with a man who does not frankly recognise the presence of spiritual force in the world.

And thus it is that the story of Nicodemus, when we put it into our modern ways of speech, turns out to be a very common story. We meet it every day. Surely, men tell us, when we are viewing the religion of Christ, we are viewing what is a natural fact, and we must treat it like other facts. There is a good deal in it that is true, no doubt; but do not let us set up any extravagant claims for it. Let us be cautious, like Nicodemus; above all things, let us have regard to the claims of common sense. But the answer of our Lord is decisive. "What is born of the flesh is flesh, but what is born of the Spirit is spirit." You cannot understand the first principles of the Christian creed unless you are prepared to accept the spiritual in some form. And, if you recognise it in one direction, you need not marvel if you are called to recognise it in others. For the root of the matter is this, that the grace of the Incarnation offers new energies, new powers, which are so far-reaching in their effects that the acquisition of them is a true regeneration. And this grace is not anything we can claim as part of our intellectual inheritance as members of the human family—it is God's gift. It is no more unphilosophical or unscientific to recognise the presence and the power of the grace of Christ playing upon our lives, than it is to recognise the reality of spiritual force in general. It is only an intellectual timidity which restrains us, as it restrained Nicodemus, from welcoming the doctrines of grace. We are afraid of being branded as extravagant or as mystical. We fear that we shall be set down as narrow dogmatists, if we glory in the gifts which Christ is ready to give. There is, perhaps, no form of caution more common than this, which prevents men from pressing to their inevitable conclusion in logic the fact that Christianity is a supernatural system which derives its life from the incarnation of the Son of God. It is right, indeed—there is hardly any need to say it—to be cautious up to a certain point; but in speculation, as in practice, an excessive caution will check all progress and paralyse all effort. The words which Shakespeare puts into the mouth of his great Cardinal apply to thought as well as to life:—

> "If we shall stand still,
> In fear our motion will be mocked or carped at,
> We should take root here where we sit, or sit
> State-statues only."*

We have reached this point. The conversation of Nicodemus with our Lord is a type of the struggle of a soul. The difficulties of belief at first seem overwhelming; but they fade away and finally disappear as it becomes increasingly apparent that after all mystery meets us in every quarter once we begin to contemplate the spiritual world. Let us, then, be ready to face Christianity as men should face it who already believe in the possibility of spiritual life, who believe that the soul is not the mere outcome of physical antecedents, but that it is capable of intercourse with Him in whose image we are made. So believing, whatever we may decide as to difficult points of Christian doctrine, we shall, at least, not dare to ask the question of Nicodemus, "How can these things be?" That they are possible is involved at once in the character of God and the needs of the human soul.

And once again. "That which is born of the

* *Henry VIII.*, Act I., Sc II.

Spirit is spirit." No one who has even imperfectly grasped the fact of the Incarnation will venture to speak of Christianity as if it were a mere body of doctrines, justified to the intellect by what are called evidences. It is a great deal more than this. It is a system of life, as well as of doctrine. And a fruitful source of theological controversy is that this is ignored. Arguments are sometimes used which entirely overlook the fact that Christianity is nothing if not supernatural, and that its supernatural character is manifested not only by the stupendous occurrences with which it was ushered into the world, but by the supernatural graces which it yet has to offer. "Except a man be born of water and the Spirit, he cannot enter into the kingdom of God."* "Except ye eat the flesh of the Son of Man and drink His blood, ye have not life in yourselves."† In these words of Christ the power of baptismal and of eucharistic grace is spoken of as plainly as we could desire. Let us not mistake the issue. Either Christ did not tell us the truth, or the Gospel of the Incarnation has a message to us still. That the vision of the divine kingdom is pledged only to the regenerate, ceases to be a maxim of spiritual exclusiveness when we remember that in the same breath regeneration is promised to all those who

* St. John iii. 5.   † St. John vi. 53.

have been baptized into the Christian name. The blessings of the Incarnation are with us, and affect us even now whether we desire it or not; it is ours only, with God's help, so to put them to right use in this world that we lose them not finally in the life to come. Do we say that such a belief is too good to be true? God forbid. To say that anything is too good to be true, when we are thinking of God's gifts, is treason against Him. Nothing is too good to be true* for him who believes that the source of all goodness is the eternal and unchangeable Truth. For "the greatness of His mercy reacheth unto the heavens even as His truth unto the clouds."

* George Eliot says, in a letter to Miss Hennell: "There is a sort of blasphemy in saying that a thing is too good to be true."

EVOLUTION AND THE DOCTRINE OF THE INCARNATION.

"The first man Adam was made a living soul; the last Adam was made a quickening spirit."—1 Cor. xv. 45.

Preached before the University of Dublin,
Second Sunday in Lent, 1893

EVOLUTION AND THE DOCTRINE OF THE INCARNATION.

THE contrast here instituted by St. Paul between Adam and our Lord is familiar, and it suggests many thoughts which it would be interesting to expand. Viewing his words quite literally, without any backward glance at the teaching of science as to the gradual development of the human race from ruder and less perfect types, they seem to teach us that the crisis in human history which we call the Incarnation had results even farther reaching than the crisis of Creation. "The first Adam was made a living soul; the last Adam was made a life-giving spirit." The first Adam received a gift. The second bestowed one. And the constant teaching of St. Paul is that the unique relation of our Lord to us is to be sought not only in the beauty of His moral precepts, in the example of His blameless life, but in that divine force which He imparted to the whole human race when He took human flesh upon Himself. The Incarnation is not like a passing event in the history of the world; it is "an eternal fact in the divine life" by which all human life is affected, inasmuch as a new source of moral energy is thus made available for men.

This is an aspect of truth which, I believe, we are sometimes tempted to pass by. The teaching of science as to the order of nature, and the regularity of nature's working, makes us impatient of any speculation which seems to hint that the progress of the race has not been always continuous. The law of continuity, indeed, has been often treated as if it were not merely a convenient principle for guidance, but an absolute principle of nature. And thus it has been urged that we must not tolerate the assumption of any break in the development of man. His growth has really, we are told, been quite uniform. Evolved from rude types in the remote past, he has gradually reached the stage at which we now see him, the stage at which he possesses self-conscious reason and a responsible will. And, as to his religion, to suppose that Christianity has any higher claim upon our allegiance than the claim that it has in virtue of its being the last product of human endeavour to pierce the veil between us and the unseen world, is to shut our eyes to the fact that like all religions, it has a history of its own which may be traced. To suppose that there is any finality about it, nay, to suppose that there is anything unique about it, is only a mark of that amiable weakness which always leads us to put a high value on what is specially our own.

I propose to consider, then, what light is thrown on the doctrine of the Incarnation by the teaching of science as to the gradual character of human development. And first we observe that, as a crisis in human history, St. Paul compares—for his contrast involves a comparison—the incarnation of our Lord with the creation of man. What has science to tell us about the latter fact? It will be sufficient for our present purpose to note that, while it forbids us to believe that man is an excrescence upon the face of creation, a being out of all natural relation to the other animals by which he is surrounded, it does not, it cannot, tell us that he is not possessed of a unique faculty. His bodily organism is, if you will, developed by the strictest process of natural law out of lower and less complex organisms; but science is going beyond what it can legitimately maintain, if it asserts that his mental and moral powers have been thus explained.

Perhaps we may put the case somewhat thus. If we could trace the curve of development of the human race from its beginnings, we should find somewhere upon it a critical point, after which a new character is assumed. That is the point of which Scripture speaks when it tells us that man was made "in the image of God." However imperfectly we may be able to grasp the full meaning of this phrase, we can see at least that it points to the acquisition by human beings of certain powers hitherto beyond their reach. When the race had reached that stage of development at which it was fitted to receive the gift, the gift was granted. When the need arose, it was supplied. The lower animals may be never so closely allied with man, and yet may be without this his peculiar privilege, because they could not appreciate it, if offered. Their organism may be incapable of responding to the demands that would be made upon it by such a faculty as self-conscious reason or deliberate will. The gift was only given to the race when the race was ready. It was given "in the fulness of time."

But that is the Christian view of the matter. Is there any objection to it on the part of science? The objection usually urged is that a breach of continuity is here implied, and that to speak of any gaps in the steady growth of nature is unscientific. And such an objection has its force, but its force is much lessened, if not altogether removed, by certain considerations which we will do well to bear in mind.

In the first place, as has been said already, the law of continuity is not a fetish before which we must bow down and worship. It is a principle of scientific investigation, but not on that account an unvarying law of nature. And if we remember that physical formulæ are not wanting in which discontinuity is plainly involved, we shall be slow to deny that there may be points on the curve of development of the human species at which the character of the curvature abruptly changes. If the facts are not fully accounted for by the hypothesis of continuous growth, there is nothing unscientific in rejecting it as inadequate.

And in the next place he would be a rash man who would assert with confidence that the Christian theory of the evolution of man involves real and not only apparent discontinuity. To speak of what did or did not happen in these remote ages of the past as if we knew all the facts of the case, is in the highest degree presumptuous. To the Divine Mind the whole growth of the human race, of the earth, of the solar system, may be marked by the most unvarying principles, but we, who only see "as in a glass, darkly," are here and there brought up short by facts which we cannot reduce to law. To borrow an illustration which may be admissible in a University pulpit. Mathematicians tell us that there are many curves made up of isolated points, in addition to a continuous curved line. To a non-mathematical mind it seems an absurd paradox to maintain that a single outlying point can be treated as lying on a continuous curve in its neighbourhood. But, in spite of the apparent absurdity, nothing is more certain than that it can be so treated. A curve, which to the eye appears to be discontinuous and broken, is known by the mathematician to follow an unvarying law. Now it is not Agnosticism, but common sense, to suppose that our knowledge is at least as inferior to that of the Divine Mind, as the knowledge of geometry possessed by the beginner is inferior to the knowledge of the skilled mathematician. In short, apparent discontinuity may not involve any real breach of law; and indeed the whole progress of science tends to bring what were formerly outstanding and anomalous facts under the protection of general principles.

When we compare, then, the Christian revelation that man was made " in the image of God " with the teaching of science, we find ourselves constrained to depict the curve of progress of the human race in its early stages as a continuous curve with a remarkable critical point. The growth was, on the whole, uniform, but a new power, a new life, was introduced at a certain stage, introduced when, and only when, man became capable of receiving it.

Considerations such as these seem to help us to understand better St. Paul's words, and to give fresh point and force to the comparison suggested in the text. "The first Adam was made a living soul; the second Adam a life-giving spirit."

The Incarnation marks a crisis in the history of human life. To the first Adam all the previous history of the animal creation may be said to point. It leads up to man, as its goal and final cause. And so with the second Head of the human race. The divine purpose in creation was, we may well believe, that human nature might be raised to its perfection by being brought into union with God. And to Christ as "the Word," who "became flesh," all the previous history of mankind, Jew and Gentile, Greek and barbarian, pointed, and for Him it prepared the way.

And again, as with the first Adam, so with the second. He came "in the fulness of time," at that precise moment when the human race was ready for Him. Within the circle of Judaism, "the law," as St. Paul assures us, "was a schoolmaster to lead men to Christ." And it is a familiar thought that even beyond the borders of the Hebrew people, we may trace in the training of the other great nations of antiquity a discipline preparatory to the Christian revelation. But still, as with the first Adam, so with the second. The development which prepared could not produce. Christ is not the mere product of the age and country in which He appeared. If He is the Son of Man, He is "the Son of Man which is in heaven." In the fact that man was made "in the image of God" we may perhaps see something which, humanly speaking, rendered possible the subsequent assumption of man's nature by the Eternal Word. But, however that may be, this we know, that the Incarnation, like the Creation, was not a mere result of development. It was a fresh crisis.

Thus, when the "first Adam was made a living soul," the race was endowed with gifts which were in no sense results of its past growth. And the like may be said of the gifts of Christ. We entirely mistake the position of Christianity as the absolute religion if we fail to observe that our Lord claims to be not only "the way and the truth," but also "the life." He puts new possibilities of spiritual achievement within our reach. In Him, as in Adam, a new source of spiritual energy is made accessible; though there is a sense, as St. Paul points out, in which there is a contrast as well as a comparison. For the gifts of Christ are given not only "in" His person, but "through" His person. He is a "life-giving spirit," and not only a "living soul."

Again these gifts, as we have seen, were not granted until man was in a position to use them. They were not granted when man was in a state of primitive innocence and purity. His nature, as it seems, was not developed sufficiently to profit by them. Long years of growth, of discipline—possibly rendered longer by that backward step in human history which we call the Fall—long periods of training were needed before man could appreciate the perfect gifts which were in store. And to mention one further point of comparison and one only. The gifts given to the human race in the person of Adam were given in perpetuity. The race has not lost them. So too the Incarnation brings its gifts to mankind, new endowments, new energy, which we may neglect, but which we cannot get rid of. The responsibilities of humanity were permanently increased as truly at the crisis of the Incarnation as at the crisis of Creation.

We may well ask ourselves what are the practical issues involved in such a conception of our heritage as alike the sons of Adam and the sons of God. The issues are momentous indeed. Our attitude in regard to the Christian Church, our conception of present duty, our hopes of an eternal future, are all affected by the truth that God became man and thenceforward has never left man to himself.

Our view of the Church is affected by it. The incarnation of the Son of God, which brought fresh vigour to a weary race, is even now the source of the life of the Christian Church. The Christian Church is sometimes spoken of as if it were nothing but a widely extended and respectable society established for the purpose of promoting Christian knowledge. This indeed it is, but unless it is something more, then were the most cherished convictions of the apostles but delusions, nay, then was St. Paul entirely mistaken when he compared our Lord's incarnation to the beginnings of self-conscious life on the globe. The Incarnation is a perpetual spring of life; that we can never repeat to ourselves too often. And the Church which the Lord set up on earth is the custodian and the dispenser of the divine gifts thus placed within the reach of men, who (as we confess in the collect) "have no power of themselves to help themselves." We cannot say indeed that the consequences of that wonderful fact do not extend far beyond the limits of Christendom, beyond the pale of the Catholic Church. The channels of God's grace are manifold; no man dare circumscribe them. But this we can say, that it is only the Christian society that is empowered to offer these gifts to "all sorts and conditions of men." It is only because of the Incarnation and through the Incarnation that there is any efficacy in sacraments. We need not trouble ourselves with vexed questions as to the mode of operation of sacramental grace. The really important thing for us to hold fast is that Christ offers us in His Church gifts which are in no sense the natural and necessary endowments of humanity. Indeed, if we only look far enough back, we may see that we cannot claim from the circumstances of our pedigree even such common faculties as self-conscious reason and the power of choice. They are, to use at once the simplest and truest words, the gift of God. And through these gifts we are enabled to benefit by those others which Christ offers us in the sacramental system of His Church. "The last Adam was made a life-giving spirit," not only at the moment of incarnation, but in perpetuity through the channel of the society of which He is the head, that society which is the true home of grace.

This conclusion affects our conception of present duty. We are responsible for the right use of these gifts. The curve of development of the human race seems now, as far as man may judge, to have been continuous for close upon nineteen centuries. But the history of the past teaches us that these periods of continuous growth are periods of discipline. It is in them that the world's training is carried on. A higher gift is never offered until the lower gift has been appreciated. And so it is that we are all being trained, even now, in the manifold discipline of life, that we may be worthy at last to receive those " good gifts which God hath prepared for them that love Him." There is, indeed, no compulsion put upon us. We may despise our natural heritage as men. We may, like Esau, give up our birthright of the higher life in obedience to the promptings of that part of our nature which we have in common with the brute. And so, too, we may give up our birthright as Christian men who, as baptized into the name of Christ, have an interest in the gifts of the Incarnation. All of which God forbid! for in very deed in both cases is that true which St. Paul says to us in the Epistle for to-day, " He therefore that despiseth, despiseth not man but God."

But we cannot think of the present life as a discipline without letting our thoughts travel forward. It is a discipline; and we ask, a discipline for what? We can give no detailed answer. There are, indeed, hints in Scripture that once more there will be a turning point in the history of humanity, when the gifts of the Incarnation have been put to right use, when sin has been conquered, when we have learnt to realise that life in Christ of which the apostles speak with such certainty and such joy. The seer of the Apocalypse speaks of " a new heaven and a new earth" which are to continue after " the former things have passed away." Once more a critical point, and then an endless progress—a progress in that knowledge of God which is eternal life. More we do not know. Enough to feel that "now are we the sons of God, though it doth not yet appear what we shall be."

CHRIST THE TRUTH.

"I am . . . the Truth."—St. John xiv. 6. &

Preached before the University of Oxford,
Twenty-second Sunday after Trinity, 1894.

CHRIST THE TRUTH.

THERE have been periods in Christian history when those who rejected the claims of Christ thought it incumbent on them to insist that His teaching was injurious to the welfare of the human race, that it was not only useless but positively harmful, that it was not only incomplete but untrue. The attack upon Christianity made by Celsus in the second century, which has secured its permanent place in history through the masterly reply of Origen, was, to speak generally, of this character. The controversial fables disseminated by zealous Jews of which we read in early Christian literature seem to have been inspired with the idea that Christ was nothing more than a false prophet, whose miracles were to be accounted for by the arts of magic. And —to instance only one other period when a like tendency displayed itself—at the close of the eighteenth century the ill-considered materialism which for the moment seemed to have mastered the best spirits both in England and France, declared that the old twilight of Christian prejudice was to be replaced in the near future by the clear and dry light of reason. Christianity was a fable; Christ a false teacher.

In our own day serious persons do not so speak. Among the educated classes there are few indeed who would commit themselves to the doctrine that there was *no* truth in the teaching of the Founder of Christianity. For, at any rate, Christianity has lived, and has been the strength and stay of the civilised world for many centuries, and a lie cannot live or bring forth such goodly fruits. No! that Christianity is not without an element of truth, that the Sermon on the Mount contains precepts full of the highest wisdom, that individual Christians govern their lives well in proportion as they follow the commands of their Master, all this the world is ready enough to admit. And those who are most anxious to replace the religion of Jesus by other forms of faith and worship which seem to them better suited to the needs of civilised humanity, are the most ready to acknowledge with gratitude that the discipline of the Christian centuries has not been without precious result. The law was a schoolmaster to lead men to Christ; and—at the least—Christ has been a schoolmaster to lead men to that higher and more fully developed religion which, it seems, mankind requires and seeks.

The banner of the cross, then, has triumphed to this extent that its foes no longer treat it with insult or contumely; they are willing that it should be placed, as a venerable monument of antiquity, in that museum of comparative religion which is to be reared on the ruins of the Christian cathedral. Christianity is allowed to have been the exponent of *some* truths. No one any longer cares to speak slightingly of its origin, however lightly he may think of its destiny in the rational and highly educated ages of the future.

To believe, however, that Christianity contains a great deal of truth is not to believe in Christ. For our Lord asserts, in the startling words of the text, not only that He is a wise Teacher, not only that His precepts are true, not only that He Himself embodies certain aspects of truth, but that He is *the* Truth, that He includes all that has been, or is, or can be known; nothing short of this is the claim He makes. And it is precisely here that many minds find a difficulty in their allegiance. Surely—it is said—there are many sides of truth, historical or scientific, which religion does not touch at all; surely, again, there are certain elements of truth to be found in the non-Christian religions of the world.

To press the words, "I am the Truth," in their literal meaning is to claim that Christianity has a monopoly of truth, and that is a claim of which no one who thinks will be likely to admit the justice.

Such a criticism—a criticism which is often heard —is not without foundation. It might be pointed out of course, that the words of the text are in no way inconsistent with the belief that in other creeds are enshrined many precious fragments of truth; though, indeed, he who believes Christ to be the way as well as the truth will be tempted to follow the old Greek theologians in regarding the pre-Christian religions as affected, though unconsciously, by that divine Logos of whom every race of man partakes. But not to dwell upon this, which is not necessarily connected with our present subject, we may go further and admit fully and frankly that the Christian creeds, as understood and expanded at any one time do not contain all the truth. They may have—they have— proved amply sufficient to inspire and invigorate mankind, but there must be certain aspects of truth which have not yet come directly within their purview. For it is one thing to say that a formula contains explicitly all that is true or that can be known ; it is quite another thing to say that a Person is Himself the eternal and unchangeable and universal

Truth. It is this latter which Christ claims for Himself, which His Church vindicates for Him. And it is worth our while to observe how this is involved in the very statement of the fact of the Incarnation. Abstract reasoning will not, indeed, get us very far in this high and difficult subject. We need to walk reverently as we enter the sanctuary of the sacred edifice of Christian doctrine. But it is instructive to remind ourselves at times of the conclusions to which the best thought of the Church has tended.

"I am the Truth," said Christ. Our attitude in respect of that saying of His is determined by our belief as to His person. If He were not the Son of God as well as the Son of Man, there would be no profit in discussing so tremendous a claim. The sons of men are limited in their faculties, in their judgment, in their acquirements; the wiser they are, the better they know how faulty their judgments are likely to be, how small is the range of their knowledge. But we who believe Jesus the Son of Mary to be Himself the Eternal Word, must consider His claims in the light of the Incarnation. And it seems to be revealed in Scripture, and accepted by the Church, that God in becoming man took upon Him the nature of humanity at large, that He united to Himself not the personality of a favoured individual, but the nature of the race. Thus He represents in

Himself all men, past, present, and to come, with their gifts and their achievements no less than their troubles and their tears.* And not the nature of man alone, for we are now beginning to learn the meaning of St. Paul's phrase that Christ is the "first born of all creation." Man is not isolated in the universe, an afterthought of the Creator; nay, he is the flower and the crown of creation. He is that to which nature points, to which the forces of life gradually lead. His nature, viewed on the side of its origin, is not disconnected from that of the rest of the animal world. And so the Incarnation acquires a cosmical significance; it seems to have far wider relations than those in which men are immediately concerned. It affects all created life. The Eternal Word, "by whom all things were made," has entered into yet more intimate union with His creation. So it is that Christ is "the Truth." He who recapitulates and sums up mankind in His person is also— perhaps we may dare to say, is therefore—the representative of all creation.

And this, we may be sure of it, is no barren speculation. It bears on the practical problems which in some form or other we all have to face. For the issue is this: Either Christ is not true, or He is *the* Truth; either the religion of the Incarnation is

* Compare Irenæus *contra Haer.* III. xxii. 3.

CHRIST THE TRUTH. 71

inconsistent with its own first principle, or it must be concerned with every interest of our manifold life. Let me venture to remind you of some directions in which this thought may be of practical service.

And, first, if we remember that Christ is the Truth, we shall be saved from any misgivings, such as are felt from time to time even by Christian people, as to the advantage or propriety of substituting Christianity for the heathen religions of those inferior races to whom we are responsible in virtue of conquest. If Christianity only contained fragments of truth, it might be plausibly argued that it should not be pressed upon those to whom it did not appeal immediately and of itself. But if Christ be "the Truth," we dare not refrain from proclaiming Him and His message to mankind. That there are elements of truth in the religions of the non-Christian world no thoughtful person will dare to deny; we gladly and thankfully recognise that the Eternal has never "left Himself without a witness" among men. But a half truth is often more misleading than a direct lie. Truths taken out of their context and misapplied are mischievous indeed. No apology is needed for the effort to bring unity and coherence into what is unsystematic and disorderly; and that is, in part, what the Christian missionary claims to do with the religions of heathendom. In the past it has been not only by condemnation of the false, but by appropriation of the true, that Christianity has won its triumphs. So it must be still; for to work thus is to work in the spirit of Him who came " not to destroy the law but to fulfil." And it is when working in such a spirit that we realise most intensely that Christ could not be the Truth for us were He not the Truth for all.*

Or, again, to those who thus view the Gospel, any separation between the religious and the secular life will seem an unnatural divorce. The problems of life are all problems of Christianity, for Christianity is the expression of the principle that Christ unifies and hallows all life. The day is gone by— let us pray that it may never return—when it was thought unworthy of a minister of the Gospel to busy himself in such secular matters as the housing of the poor, or the strife between capital and labour. Nay! Christ is "the Truth." If we cannot learn from Him the solution of all our problems, social and national as well as individual, problems of practice and problems of theory, the fault is ours not His. Again I say, the point is not that Christianity claims

---

* Compare the question in the *Stromata* (p. 298) of Clement of Alexandria : πῶς δ'ἄν ἰστι σωτῆρ καὶ κύριος εἰ μὴ πάντων σωτῆρ καὶ κύριος;

to occupy all the fields of human activity, but that it *must* occupy them if it be true at all and not a dream which but cheats us with the semblance of reality.

And yet again, it is because Christ is the Truth that His Church welcomes—there is no need to say it in Oxford—every addition to the sum of knowledge, whether historical or scientific. It is without any unworthy fear that she views the investigations made in the name and for the sake of truth, for she recognises that thus even those who do not rank themselves under the banner of the cross are doing the work, though they know it not, of the Crucified. "All truth," as St. Augustine says, "comes from Him who said I am the Truth." "We can do nothing," says St. Paul, "against the truth, but for the truth."* The highest privilege of a Christian disciple is to be, in St. John's words, a "fellow-worker with the truth."†

And thus the religion of the Incarnation takes in not only the past, but the present and the future. The words of the text imply something far greater than the consistency and trustworthiness of Christ's recorded sayings. For they mean that in the person of Christ is offered not only the answer to the problems which perplex us, but the answer to the

* 2 Cor. xiii. 8. † 3 John 8.

problems—whatever they may be—which will perplex our children. Here is what philosophy has ever sought—a unifying principle of knowledge, a central fact, the knowledge of which will be implicitly the knowledge of all that can be known. The dream of the philosopher finds its realisation in the faith of the Crucified. "In Him are hid all the treasures of wisdom and knowledge." And so His revelation is the final revelation, for nothing can be greater or more than the truth.

But it will be said that such a doctrine goes perilously near to evacuating the Christian creed of any meaning. If Christianity claims to embrace the whole field of human activity, if nothing is to it "common or unclean," what is its distinctive character? Would it not be true that, as Goethe said, "he who has science and art has religion"? In the endeavour to give a religious significance to scientific investigation, is there not a danger of so confusing religion and science that the former may lose that which has given it its strength and vitality in the past? And there would be some plausibility in this objection were the object of Christian belief a series of propositions and not a Person. But it is a supreme Person who in declaring that He is the Truth has given us courage to knock at every door of knowledge, to claim the whole territory as ours, for "we are Christ's." The words "Homo sum, humani nihil a me alienum puto,"* when applied to the Son of Man, acquire a deeper meaning than was present to the mind of the Roman playwright. For it is not theories or beliefs about Christ, but Christ Himself that can be identified with the truth. And though all investigation of truth be watched with eager interest and hearty sympathy by the Christian, yet he dare not call it religious unless the seeker recognises that truth is represented and embodied in a Person. The truth must be seen in Him who is the Eternal Wisdom before it can be seen clearly and in its completeness. Thus the old question "What is truth?" is the question, Where shall we hear the voice of Jesus Christ? And the answer is, You may hear it everywhere—in the voice of external nature, in the voice of Scripture, in the voice of the Church, in the voice of conscience, and not least in the half conscious cries of the human soul which can find satisfaction in nothing less than Him. Yes, we may find truth everywhere, but we shall not grasp it in its right relation to practice unless we consciously recognise the voice which brings it to us as the voice of Jesus Christ. For, as we have often been reminded, He is indeed, "a present, living Teacher;" and His Spirit is ever at work in the world and in

* Terence, *Heautontim.* i. 1.

the Church guiding the patient and the faithful into all the truth.

We have, then, reached this point. We have seen that the Incarnation, when apprehended as an incarnation and not a mere theophany, requires us to believe that He who has become incarnate is Himself the sum of truth. We have seen, too, that this justifies us in regarding the religion of Christ as a universal religion, not only a religion for all men, but a religion which will embrace all that concerns the interests of mankind in this world and in the world to come—as a religion not only for the past but for the present and the future. And this touches some of us very closely, for it seems to suggest that as a University claims in its very title to embrace the whole field of knowledge, so its highest function is discharged when it leads men to a knowledge of Him who is Himself the Truth. *Credo ut intelligam* is the confession of a wise no less than pious soul, if we interpret it aright. I believe Christ, that He may teach me to learn.

And if we go on to ask—as we must, for this is the really important matter in practice—if we go on to ask for the conditions under which we may gain this greatest knowledge, we shall find in the conditions under which we become masters of any the least tract of science, hints enough to set us thinking.

He who would find the Truth need not be surprised if the hindrances and helps to his great enterprise are analogous to those which we experience every day in the attempt to appropriate any fragment of truth. The analogy must not be pressed too far; but it is perhaps worth while to pursue it a little way.

And, in the first place, do we not know that all knowledge worthy of the name is slowly acquired? Little indeed has our University taught us if it has not taught us that. The most precious truths are those which are hardest to learn, which every day's experience fills with a larger meaning. And this is true not only of that personal knowledge of God which is the root of all serious religion; it is true of the doctrinal knowledge of the Church at large. It is only by slow degrees that the fulness of the Gospel is revealed. It is only by slow and often painful steps that we enter into our Catholic inheritance. We are only gradually learning to interpret our charter. So it is again with the solution of those social problems of which the Gospel must indeed contain the solution, or it would not be the Gospel; but the end is not yet. We demand of the Christ a judgment, which no man shall be able to gainsay, as to the conflicting claims of brethren; but He answers us as He answered of old, "Man who made me a judge or a divider over you?"* The problems of society can only be wrought out in the friction of society, even though the society be the body of Christ. "When Messiah is come He will declare unto us all things,"† was the pious reflection of the Samaritan woman. Ay, but not in a day or a year or a generation. It is in the daily discipline of life that we slowly learn. And there are even moments when the Spirit of the Lord says to us as to Moses, "Wherefore criest thou unto me? speak unto the children of Israel that they go forward."‡ To work is to pray, and spiritual insight is gained by work as by prayer.

Knowledge, then, is gained slowly and through discipline. Is it not also true that it is best acquired not in isolation but in the life of a society? There have, no doubt, been remarkable cases of lonely workers who have done sound and enduring work, who have left the world richer than they found it. But of such men it may fairly be said that they were successful in their quest after truth in spite of, and not because of their method. For not only does the isolated student lose that counsel and sympathy of comrades, without which, to those who have enjoyed it, the world would seem poor indeed; but he is apt

---

* St. Luke xii. 14. † St. John iv. 25
‡ Exod. xiv. 15.

CHRIST THE TRUTH. 79

to lose a due sense of proportion. No man's individual experience is so wide that he can venture to regard his judgments as of universal validity; he needs the salutary restraints which are offered by the criticism of his peers. And again—what is more important—it would be sheer waste of time and strength, in the acquisition of knowledge, to begin as if we were the first to embark on the voyage of discovery after truth. Common sense itself bids us begin by following in the track of those who have gone before. We do not begin—in a University at least—with negations, but with those positive formulæ in which the sum of the world's wisdom has been expressed. We have indeed to test these by personal experience and verification. Without such testing we cannot really appropriate truth. And at times we may have to retrace our steps; at times the old formula refuses to submit to the tests which we feel bound to impose. And then we have to go through the sad and anxious process of readjusting our beliefs. But however that may be, and perhaps we are sometimes over-hasty in our attempts at readjustment, the natural order is from the verdict of society to the personal experience of the individual. Those who reverse this order, and begin as if no one had ever learnt anything before, are apt to arrive at strange results. People who propose to square the circle or to prove that the earth is flat are rarely persons who have followed what are called "traditional" methods. No! a wise man does not isolate himself or begin with a negation. It is in society that he learns, and he takes from society the accumulated experience of the past as his starting point. For he ever remembers that great a thing as it is to seek truth it is a greater thing to find it, a yet greater—yes, and a more difficult—thing to keep it.

And surely all this applies to religion. No matter how low a view we take of the Christian society, it is at least certain that the general advantages of membership of a society—be it only an ancient society for promoting Christian knowledge—are not to be despised by the earnest seeker after the truth. He will not begin as if no one had seriously considered the claims of Christ before him; he will not begin by constructing a theory of the Incarnation for himself; he will rather try to appropriate and make his own the teaching of His Church about Him who is the Truth. The creed so presented must indeed be submitted to the test and the trial of life; if it does not illumine life then we do not want it. But let us be sure, in the first instance, that we understand it aright.

So much will not be thought unreasonable by any;

but we must go a step farther. For if Christ be what He claimed to be, then is His Church the custodian of the truth in an especial sense. She made a gallant attempt in the Middle Ages to systematise all knowledge, with only partial success; though perhaps the success seems somewhat greater to students of the *Summa* than to those who pass it by as a curiosity of mediæval subtlety. But at any rate if the details were not altogether satisfactory, yet the ruling principles were sound; for are they not these, that Christianity is co-extensive with everything that concerns mankind, and that it is the privilege of the Christian Church, "the pillar and ground of the truth," to interpret to mankind the revelation which has been vouchsafed? We have been considering the first of these principles; we dare not pass by the second.

The one principle is that of the catholicity of the Christian religion, and the other—no less weighty— is that of its exclusiveness. This latter is indeed a claim which will not be so readily conceded as the former. For the former principle is agreeable to believe; it hurts no one's feelings to say that Christianity, when rightly interpreted, embodies all that is true and takes account of all the interests of mankind. But the question of right interpretation comes to the front sooner or later, and we cannot

F

dispense ourselves from seeking an answer to it. There are many rival claimants for the prophetical office. And when it is said that the Christian Church is, peculiarly and of divine right, the custodian of the truth as revealed in the person of Christ Jesus, the claim is received with scant favour, not only by the religious bodies which have broken away from historical Christianity, but by the irreligious world. Men are not unwilling to admit that in a general way Christianity embraces all truth, but they are extremely unwilling to admit that the Church has been commissioned to teach it with authority, or even that it is more likely to be learnt within than without her borders.

Let us, then, re-state for ourselves what it is that we hold to be taught in Scripture and verified in history as to the office of the Church of Christ in respect of truth. The Church is, to begin with, not to be described as a society of men who have banded themselves together for a religious object. It is not a self-constituted organisation. It was not founded by the apostles as a means of carrying on their work. It was not the offspring of a desire on the part of Christians to unite for mutual comfort and consolation. It was not set up to perpetuate the memory of a departed Master, or to study and develop His precepts of wisdom. If it had originated in any of these ways, its imperious claims would be without warrant either in history or in common sense. What is it then? It is the kingdom of God which Christ came to found, a kingdom stretching from earth to heaven, its members militant here, triumphant hereafter. It is the body of which Christ is the head, not merely the society of which He was the founder. It is a society too, but a divine society, the motto of whose life is, "Ye have not chosen me, but I have chosen you." This society, which was formed before and not after the truth had been fully revealed, is not a convenient means of keeping Christians in communion and fellowship; it is rather in virtue of their incorporation into it that they are Christians at all. And it is this society to which the guidance of the divine Spirit was pledged, that claims to be the one authoritative exponent of the truth.

Does it seem to you an extravagant claim? Consider then and weigh this undoubted fact, that the many religious sects which have sprung up from time to time in Christendom have derived their strength and their popularity from this one thing, that they have concentrated themselves on the exposition of certain fragments only of the deposit of truth, to the exclusion of whatever portion seemed to be inconsistent with prevalent theories or unsuitable to the spirit of the age. It is indeed the case that in Christianity, as represented by the various dissenting bodies, there is much that is most valuable in practice as it is most true in theory. It may be most wholesome for us to be reminded of certain portions of truth which we were letting slip, not perhaps from our creeds, but from our lives. But it is not the way to mend such a state of things, to declare that nothing is important but the one truth which has been partially forgotten.

In fact, as we have seen that the isolated individual worker is apt to lose a sense of proportion, and to estimate the importance of truth chiefly in relation to his own personal and immediate needs, so it is with all religious bodies which start with the principle of individualism. Such a society is a mere chance agglomerate of individuals who have drifted together through the beliefs which they happen to hold in common, but it does not possess any pledge of permanence, any guarantee of completeness in the teaching it offers. And such teaching is not only incomplete; it is necessarily devoid of authority. It represents a body of honest individual opinion, but it represents nothing more; while on the other hand the very first principle of the Church's teaching is, that it is not the product of the intelligence of its individual members as exercised upon a book, but that it is a deposit held in trust for all future generations, because it was first given to the world by the Eternal Truth Himself. It is this society which has, as a matter of fact, guarded the truth for you in the past, that claims to teach you in the present and the future, as you share in its common life.

And so what we have come to is this. Individual responsibility for our opinions we can never shake off; we should be unworthy of our manhood did we try to do so. But we are also responsible for the way in which we arrive at our opinions. If we are determined to begin with a negation, to live without prayer, without Christ, without sacraments, until we have made ourselves master of all that has been said by speculative persons for and against Providence, the Incarnation, the Church—then we must not be surprised if we find our creed somewhat thin and unsatisfying in after years. We need not imagine that any individual life is long enough to exhaust the secrets of the divine wisdom. But we shall not be so presumptuous as to assume that it is. We shall rather begin, as we would in any other matter, with the accumulated experience of the past, and spend the future in the honest endeavour to verify and enlarge it for ourselves And then our own poor experience shall become in its turn part of that witness which the Church shall bear to future ages. For she is taught by the Spirit no otherwise than by the operation of the Spirit on the minds of faithful men. As we listen to her voice, we shall, at least, not be like children, carried about with every blast of vain doctrine, but shall be established in the truth.

And lastly, of what nature is this highest knowledge thus slowly gained in the bosom and through the voice of a society? Is it of merely intellectual interest? Nay, it must admit of practical application. If we may reverse the mournful words in which Seneca describes the *intemperantia literarum*, which was so marked a feature of the intellectual life of his time, the words *Non scholae sed vitae discimus*,* are words that we would all fain make our own. Not for the schools, but for life are we learning. It is no mere polished formula, not even a philosophic completeness of doctrine that will satisfy, for we seek to know a Person who will solve for us all the riddles of our life. Even here, as we have seen, our most fruitful knowledge is not gained from books but from persons; the wisdom that we learn from the lips of a revered teacher is worth more than much book-learning. So is it with the knowledge of Jesus Christ. We seek to find the sum of truth, and

* Seneca, *Epistles*, 106, §§ 11, 12.

we chafe and fret because we cannot sum an infinite series; but the knowledge of an infinite Person is a greater and a more precious possession. And with life illuminated by that knowledge, we confess with gladness that it is in His light that we shall—that we do—see light.

THE REVELATION OF LIFE IN CHRIST.

"I am He that liveth, and was dead; and behold I am alive for evermore."—Rev. i. 18.

Preached in St. Patrick's Cathedral, Dublin,
at the Opening of the General Synod,
April 10, 1893.

THE REVELATION OF LIFE IN CHRIST.

DURING the season between Easter and Ascension tide, at which we have now arrived in the course of the Church's year, our gaze is directed to the person of the risen Christ. During those forty days of joyful perplexity, the Lord's disciples were from time to time encouraged and strengthened by the visible presence of their Master, as He "showed Himself alive" to them by "many infallible proofs," and taught them "the things concerning the kingdom of God."* What is the message that the history of these forty days has for us? What is the lesson of those occasional appearances of the risen Lord, recorded in the Gospels, now to a loving woman, now to two sad travellers, now to a small company of faithful disciples?

It is easy to see, and we are all familiar with the thought, that the faith of the Church would have

* Acts i. 3.

lacked the support of that appeal to facts, which she has been accustomed to make throughout the Christian centuries, had there been no such outward and visible proofs of the resurrection of the Crucified. St. Paul gives a masterly summary of the evidence which satisfied him that in the person of Jesus Christ we have to do with one who is not subject to the ordinary laws of humanity. He appeals to the testimony of eye-witnesses in a fashion which shows that he regarded it as convincing to any reasonable mind. The fact that all the witnesses were friends, not foes, does not perplex him in the least; and indeed, it is plain that this could not possibly detract from the value of their recognition of the Master whom they had lost, and, as they thought, had lost for ever. But, though this be true, we may well doubt whether the sole or even the chief office of the great fact of the Resurrection was to supply such evidence of the truth of the Gospel of the Incarnate Word. For we may observe that had the sole purpose of our Lord's resurrection been that He might convince the world of the majesty of the visitor whom it had scorned, that object would, as it seems, have been more effectually served by some glorious appearance to the people or to their rulers, some manifestation which should startle the scoffing soldiers, the time-serving Pilate, the malicious priests.

When He rose (it is the objection of an unbeliever of the second century)* He ought to have appeared to the very persons that had insulted Him, to the judges who condemned Him, and, indeed, to all men without distinction. But nothing of the kind took place. Here the Lord showed Himself to Mary of Magdala, there to St. Peter, now to five hundred brethren at once, now to the eleven as they sat at meat, now on the shore of the sea of Galilee, now in the upper chamber at Jerusalem. But in no case where He showed Himself, so far as the sacred records inform us, during that mysterious interlude in His risen life, did He manifest His presence to those who denied His claims, or who neglected His message. The vision of the risen Christ was not for the contemptuous Roman, the sceptical Sadducee, the cruel multitude, but for His faithful and sorrowing friends.

Nor will this appear strange to us if we recall what the Gospels teach us about the general method of revelation. God does not force truth upon men. Rarely, indeed, does He teach us anything so plainly or so convincingly, that we cannot resist its entrance into our hearts if we will. There is no principle of

* See Origen, c. Celsum, ii. 63. Origen remarks in reply that it is no more matter for astonishment that the Lord did not appear to all after His resurrection, than that He did not permit all His apostles to be witnesses of His transfiguration.

religion explained more clearly in the Gospels than this, that to appreciate religious truth a certain tone of mind, a certain habit of thought, is necessary. We must be in a state of preparedness, or we shall not see the vision of God. "Repent ye," cried the Baptist, "for the kingdom of heaven is at hand."* If you do not repent, he seems to say, you will not be able to recognise that kingdom when it comes. If this were not so, it would be hard to see wherein the especial virtue of faith would lie. There is no merit in assenting to the conclusion of a train of reasoning of which the intellect admits and can perceive the cogency at every step. Religion is not like science in this; it appeals not only to the intellect, but to the whole nature of a man, his heart and his reason alike. Its methods are not the methods, nor are its laws the laws, of pure logic. It presupposes, in those to whom its truths are addressed, a state of preparedness. Nor is this peculiar to religion; we may see it every day to be the case, once we get outside the region of abstract science. We cannot appreciate a great picture, a great poem, a great piece of music, without prolonged study and discipline, without what is called culture. A man without artistic training, as a general rule, does not understand what it is that moves other persons in a work of art which seems to

* St. Matt. iii. 2.

him to be no whit superior to fifty others, which are yet passed over by those who have a right to pronounce judgment. No truth, which is anything more than a barren statement of a fact, no great principle, can be taken in without long and patient gazing upon it—in a word, without discipline. We need to say this to ourselves sometimes in an age of hurry and bustle like the present. The impatience with which results are sought in every department of research, the eager and unseemly haste with which the tentative hypotheses of science are printed in the newspapers, the vain efforts to impart really fruitful knowledge to those who will not be at the pains of acquiring it through labour—these are but indications of a temper that will surely, unless we beware, affect the spiritual life of the nation. We can gain no prize worth the gaining unless we pay the price. "In the sweat of thy face shalt thou eat bread "* is a law of the spiritual no less than of the physical world. Oh, we cannot learn anything worth learning, we cannot know anything worth knowing, without discipline—ay, without pain! It was not to the self-satisfied Pharisees, but to the Magdalen who had watched by the cross on Good Friday, that the glory of Easter was first revealed. The resurrection of Jesus Christ was only made known as

* Gen. iii. 19.

a revelation of life to those who were ready to receive it.

We have a hint of this same principle of revelation in that strange passage in St. Mark's Gospel, where we read that on one occasion Jesus "could do no mighty work."* The explanation, as it seems, is given by St. Matthew, who tells that it was because of the unbelief of the people that the Saviour's works of mercy were then left undone. A mere wonder-work, a mere feat of omnipotence, these things were (we may not doubt) at any time within the power of the Eternal Son. But the New Testament miracles, as something more than marvels, as signs of God's love in redemption, could only appeal in their full intent and purpose to those whose hearts were ready to receive the revelation in store.

Thus, then, we may see perhaps one reason why it was only to believers that the Lord showed Himself after His resurrection. For the Resurrection, as interpreted by St. Paul, is more than an evidential marvel. It is a revelation of the possibility of the life best worth living, of life in Christ. And such a possibility could not be understood, nor would such a life be desired, by one who had not yet begun to ask the meaning of a "death to sin." Thus the risen Christ appeared only to those

* St. Mark vi. 5. Cf. St. Matt. xiii. 58.

who had grieved with His grief, who knew something already of communion with Him, to those who were faithful and true. The vision of God was given only to the pure in heart. And we must surely see that so it is still. "To him that hath, to him shall be given,"* is a law of the life of grace. It is not to the careless or indifferent, not to satisfy empty curiosity or to gratify spiritual pride, that the Lord gives tokens of His presence.

Brethren, if there be any of us in this vast congregation whom the Easter message has in no way touched, who pass by and heed not the music of Easter bells, we may be sure (and it is an awful thought) that we should in like manner have passed by the Lord Himself and known Him not during that forty days of His post-resurrection life. Do we say that if we got any such convincing proofs of His claims as were then vouchsafed we should bow in adoration before Him, and consecrate the rest of our lives to His service with glad self-abandonment? Ah! are we so sure? The recognition of the risen Saviour requires faith. It is not recorded that the hireling soldiers who guarded the tomb saw anything of that manifestation of His power over death. Of the eleven favoured ones who were permitted to see their risen Lord in Galilee at the mountain where

* St. Matt. xiii. 12.

Jesus had appointed them, some, indeed, when they saw, "worshipped; but some doubted."* Even the faithful Magdalen, even the two disciples on the way to Emmaus, did not recognise Him all at once. Such glad recognition is gradual, and it is vouchsafed in proportion to the measure of our love. If we, too, would have the vision of the Christ, we must in patience and in faith keep looking back to the cross.

The revelation of the risen Lord is, then, a test of faith. But it is yet more. It is a pledge of truth, of the greatest of all truths; it is a pledge of the reality and permanence of the Incarnation. And this we cannot pass by. The message of Easter is to be regarded as essentially a revelation, as being the substance as well as the confirmation of the Gospel, because it assures us of the permanence of the incarnation of the Son of God. Jesus is "the first, and the last, and the Living One: He was dead, and behold, He is living for evermore." God is still man. Our blessed Lord did not only take our nature upon Him for a few short years of pain, and then abandon that humanity which He had assumed. No; humanity has been in Him taken for ever into God. And this, be sure of it, is far more than a barren theological dogma. It is our belief in the

* St. Matt. xxviii. 17.

permanence of the Incarnation that gives force and reality to our simplest prayers; for we feel that in prayer we are speaking to and through a human heart which can be touched by human sorrows. It gives reality to our hopes of an eternal future of personal reunion with those we love. It enlarges our views of the value and the destiny of a human soul. It intensifies our penitence for past sin, as we think that He who has taken our poor humanity upon Himself is ever pleading before the throne His own perfect and all-sufficient sacrifice. It gives a larger meaning and more gracious significance to the sacraments of the Church of God to remember that He who "dwelt among us" is still the "Word made flesh," "full of grace and truth."* God has not abandoned the human nature He assumed.

We do well at times to draw our attention from smaller issues and concentrate our gaze upon this. It is because Easter sums up all this for us that we make it the great festival of the Church's year. I say it is well to look upon this fact in its simplicity, and, so far as we can, in its fulness; for it is the centre of the Christian revelation. It is a fact of such tremendous significance that where there is agreement upon it (as there is among all Christian men), minor differences seem but the

* St. John i. 14.

differences of children who know not the seriousness of the problems which life has in store.

And we may go further. It is the very greatness of this fact, its many-sidedness, that causes differences to arise. If the Church of Christ were like an ordinary political party, based on a few simple and readily understood principles, it might be somewhat embarrassing (though perhaps not without precedent) to find Paul and Cephas and Apollos within the same fold: Paul dwelling chiefly on justification by faith, Cephas on the historical basis and setting of Christianity, Apollos on its wonderful agreement with the philosophy of the schools. And, no doubt, if the revelation of the risen Christ were so perfectly within the compass of man's reason, that we could not fail to understand it all perfectly if we set our minds to it with honesty and with patience, there would be something very perplexing in the differences that we see. But, just because it *is* a revelation, it must be beyond the scope of human intellect to grasp, and human language to express, in its entirety; and thus it is, as it would seem, inevitable that different modes of presenting the same fundamental truths will commend themselves to different minds. From the larger aberrations of individual extravagance we are saved by the collective voice of the Christian society, but lesser differences are perhaps a sign of vigorous life rather than of weakness. Every great truth is many-sided. Even the words of a teacher like Euripides or Shakespeare have manifold application: the lesson one generation extracts from them is far different from that derived by another, though both be true. And much more must this be the case when we set ourselves to grapple with a revelation from God to man, like that made in the person of the risen Christ. The lesson drawn by Paul of Tarsus will not be exactly the same lesson as that drawn by Peter of Galilee, and they will both differ from the lesson as it presents itself to Apollos of Alexandria; but each is a true lesson, true in part. The divine "wisdom is justified of all her children."*

Thus the Resurrection, as a revelation of life, is more than a test of faith or a pledge of truth; it is a bond of union among Christian men. It binds all of us together who profess the name of Christ to feel that the very differences which seem to separate us are largely due to the manifoldness and vitality of the revelation which we all accept. Not, indeed, that we prize less dearly those aspects of the faith which we have found most helpful to our own souls, but that we see that there may, nay, *must*, be in so plenteous a revelation stores of grace upon which we ourselves have not yet drawn.

* St. Luke vii. 35.

Is there any better thing we can ask than that this great revelation of life in Christ may sink deeper and ever deeper into our souls? We pray that it may show itself in greater faith, faith in the presence of the risen Christ with the Church, which is His body: in brighter hopefulness, as we remember that, though the times be dangerous, and dark clouds gather on the horizon, yet the government of the nations rests on the shoulder of One who is "the Prince of the kings of the earth:"* in larger charity, that we may, if need be, endure, suffer, believe, all things, "keeping ourselves in the love of God as we look for the mercy of our Lord Jesus Christ unto eternal life."† "Faith, hope, charity, these three;"‡ but "the greatest of these—the greatest of these is charity."

* Rev. i. 5. † Jude 21. ‡ 1 Cor. xiii. 13.

THE EDUCATION OF THE FAITHFUL.

"He shall teach you all things."—St. John xiv. 26.

Preached before the University of Dublin,
Sunday after Ascension Day, 1890.

THE EDUCATION OF THE FAITHFUL.

IN our prayers at this season that the exalting and strengthening gift of the Comforter may be continued to the Church on earth, a too often forgotten principle of religion seems to be involved —the principle that spiritual life, like physical life, is necessarily a process of growth. That life involves growth in the animal world is matter of common experience. Throughout the whole of organic nature inactivity means death; there is no such thing as stationary life. Every individual, in so far as it is endued with life, is ever changing, changing its structure and its condition; the cessation of this process would mean that its organic character was gone—that it was no longer living, but dead. And, if the conclusions of natural science as to the evolution of species one from another be considered as satisfactorily established, the same holds good not only of individuals, but of classes.

The life of a species is not so uniform and constant as it seems to observers who are but creatures of a day; new faculties and new methods of action are ever being developed, and it is in this process that the life of a species consists. Nor is there anything startling in such a doctrine to any one who believes that the Creator takes more than an occasional and transient interest in His creation, who believes rather that He is never absent from nature, but continuously governs its energies and its forces. That God guides the struggles of the meanest creature towards a higher form of existence, and directs the growth of species in their development of new capacities in the race of life—this is entirely consonant with the revealed maxim that "every good gift and every perfect gift is from above."* Nor is this now a matter of dispute; though the time is not long past when religious men deemed it a point of honour to look coldly on the instruction as to the methods of natural government which science has been able to offer us. That all truth must come from Him who said, "I am the Truth," and that nothing can ever prevail against it, as nothing can ever prevail against Him, this is a lesson we have learnt at least in part.

But we turn to the field of morals and of religion, and we find still a strange unwillingness to

* St. James i. 17.

listen to the evidence which is there being accumulated of the same great law. That the moral education of a nation as of an individual requires time; that the moral condition of a people depends largely upon their surroundings; that their moral life is a continual process of change; and that the moral character of any great historical development is to be estimated not by its poor and mean beginnings, but by its end, that to which it constantly tended—this also is true, and we dare not overlook it. Illustrations readily occur. We read of the extermination of the Canaanites, of the murder of Sisera, of the proposed sacrifice of Isaac; we listen to the cruel voices which make themselves heard in the Psalter itself; and our first impulse is to ask, Are these things pleasing to that Judge of all the earth who doeth right? But the lesson which natural science has taught us will serve us here. How do we judge of the beneficial character of a development of species in the animal world? Not surely from its beginning, but from its consummation. We do not ask, What did it begin from? but, How did it end? And in like manner, as we look back on the history of Israel, we find that the morality which was finally produced under the divine education of the people was the highest the world had ever seen. The times of Abraham, of Jael, of Joshua, were times in which the moral life of Israel was only gradually emerging from the depths of iniquity to which the neighbouring nations had sunk; we only judge fairly of the morality of the dispensation under which Israel was governed when we look at the result to which, in the course of centuries, it tended. So, turning our gaze upon that consummation, we shall pronounce it "very good."*

Whatever we may be inclined to think of sudden moral conversions in the case of individual men and women, it is plain, from the records of Holy Scripture, that the moral life of a people, under the divine leading, proceeds by slow and painful steps. It is analogous to the growth of the oak from the acorn, "unseen yet crescive in its faculty"; it is no artificial product manufactured in haste. In moral education "the old order changeth, yielding place to new"; but this process, a Christian will believe, is not blind or without purpose; it is the manifestation of a God who reveals Himself "at sundry times and in divers fashions."†

The growth of conscience, that faculty by which men learn the great laws of good and evil, is, then, divinely ordered. Is there not a similar growth to be observed in the faculties by which men apprehend

* Cf. Mozley, *Ruling Ideas in Early Ages*, Lecture x.
† Heb. i. 1.

their relation to God, the Author of goodness, and through which the divine voice is heard speaking to them? Surely the lesson of the Church to us at Ascensiontide is that this also is true. That religious life is a growth will indeed be evident to any one who reflects either on his own mental past or on the various phases which the faith has assumed in different periods of Christian-history. As our blessed Lord daily increased not only "in wisdom and in stature," but also "in favour with God and man,"* so the religious life of His Church and its faithful members alike displays growth.

And the reasons for this we shall the better appreciate if we consider first, the influence of time and circumstance upon our religion, in so far as religion is a matter of the emotions, and secondly, the effect of experience and education in relation to the formal expression of dogma.

First, then, viewed from its emotional side as an affair not only of the reason but of the heart, religion implies above all communion with a person. This has been an essential element in all religions worthy of the name; it is especially prominent in Christianity, which claims in the Incarnate Christ to have brought man nearer to God, and so to have rendered communion between the creature and the

* St. Luke ii. 52.

Creator more natural, so to speak, to mankind. Now the knowledge of a person is unlike the knowledge of a fact in this respect that emotion enters largely into it. The emotions of trust, loyalty, love—all these in turn inspire us in our intercourse with a friend whose intimacy we cherish. But the force of these emotions, from their very nature, is not constant; they vary with every variation in the circumstances of life. The feelings with which we regard a friend when sustained by his sympathy under the shock of a great sorrow are very different from those which the joy of his presence inspires when all is well with us. And we cannot be said to know a friend completely until we have made trial of his friendship in sorrow as well as in joy, until we have tested and tried his fidelity when others turn their back on us, as well as when we are basking in the sunshine of the world's favour. But this means that the consciousness of friendship continually changes its character in relation to our needs as they severally press upon us. If our friend is found faithless, it becomes cold; if he remain loyal, it is quickened and intensified. As new aspects of his character arise before us, new emotions are excited, and the answering devotion of a grateful heart goes out to him. Something like this would be the course of an ideal friendship, and if our communion with God be a reality, something analogous to it must be experienced. In time of sorrow Christ will reveal Himself as the great Consoler, in time of perplexity as the great Teacher, in time of penitence for sin as the Saviour of the soul. He changes not, but we change; and in our religious life, if it be life at all and not death, fresh aspects of His person will present themselves to our varying moods. The prayers that satisfy to-day will not satisfy to-morrow; those that were sufficient for our childish wants and learnt at a mother's knee are now put away, and greater blessings are sought. "When I was a child, I spake as a child, I understood as a child, I thought as a child, but," says the Apostle in a fragment of autobiography which appeals to all, "when I became a man I put away childish things."*

So far, then, is spiritual life a growth, that the vision of God which is promised to the pure in heart is a vision that changes its appearance in correspondence with the varying needs of men. But not only is it true that change is a feature of that emotional life of religion which is proverbially fickle; there is a growth, too, on the intellectual side. It might seem at first sight as if growth were here precluded by the crystallizing effect of language. The tendency to express our religious conceptions in words is irre-

* 1 Cor. xiii. 12.

sistible; we cannot avoid formulating them for our own protection as much as for the purpose of communicating them to others. And though it might appear as if finality were thus guaranteed, yet is it not so. The intellectual aspect of any religion which is a living force in the world changes from age to age. For, in the first place, the questions which force themselves upon the religious consciousness are not always the same. To have advanced far enough to be able to state with precision a question which is troubling us is to have gone a long way towards its solution. In an earlier stage the need for an answer was not pressing, because the question was not consciously present to thought. For example, to ask what was the doctrine of the Christian writers of the sub-apostolic age as to the mystery of the atonement or the nature of sacramental grace, would be to make an historical blunder. These problems did not present themselves so early, nor was the need of a theory felt for a long time. So, in like manner, to go yet further back, to ask what was the verdict of Greek philosophy as to the personality of God would be to make a similar blunder, for the problem of personality is a comparatively modern one, and its importance was not perceived even by the subtle intellects of Greece and Alexandria.

We may see, then, that the intellectual aspect of

religion is constantly changing, if we observe that the questions which men ask vary from century to century. Few vex themselves now with the puzzles of predestination and free-will, and yet it is not long since they convulsed religious thought in Europe; while many of the problems that are agitating men's minds to-day did not come into prominence until a few years ago.

Again, it is not only true that the questions on which the intellectual strength of the Church is concentrated vary from age to age. The answers which are given to the same question vary also, because of the necessary inability of language to keep pace with intellectual growth. We have only to take up a volume of old sermons to feel that the formulæ in which one generation enshrines its religious ideas will often utterly fail to satisfy the next. The language is not only old-fashioned, it is unreal to us. New phrases need to be devised in order to express the truths which we hold in common with our forefathers. It becomes apparent that human language is not a perfect vehicle for the transmission of a divine revelation.

But there is a far more potent cause of change than this. If the religious life of a people is at all comparable either to physical life or to moral life, there must be something more in its development than that apparent change which is accounted for by the growth of language. We have lately been told* that one of the permanent elements of religion is progress. And this must be so, because fresh light is ever being thrown on the mysteries of faith by historical research and by that better knowledge of natural law which science forces upon us. If all truth is from God, as the religious man believes, it cannot but happen that the improved moral and intellectual equipment of a people will enable them to obtain a more intelligent insight into the laws of God's spiritual kingdom. Thus with a wider education—or shall we not rather say, after a more prolonged discipline under the guidance of the Holy Ghost, the Comforter—the Church of Christ is enabled to enter more completely into the meaning of the message which she is commissioned to proclaim. That the teaching of Holy Scripture is not appreciated all at once, is shown by many conspicuous examples. Modern interpretations of the Bible are very different from those of earlier days. We do not think that Scripture bids us believe that the sun goes round the earth, as Galileo's judges did; we do not think that the first chapter of the Book of Genesis is meant to explain how the world was made out of nothing in six days of twenty-four hours each,

* The reference is to Bishop Boyd Carpenter's *Bampton Lectures*.

as Milton thought; nor, again, do we suppose that the mention of any pious man in the Bible binds our conscience to the approval of everyone of his acts, as many persons have assumed, to their own sore perplexity. Now if this be so, if these changes have taken place in the past, if the false interpretation has had to give way to the true, what reason have we for supposing that our current interpretations are final ? Absolutely none, save a belief in the infallibility of our own generation—a comfortable doctrine, but somewhat unsupported by facts. The truth is, we gather from all history, and most plainly from the history of Israel recorded for our learning, that God reveals Himself to men not all at once, but as they are able to bear it; that the possession of a divine revelation does not involve that the interpretation of it shall be free from error of detail. We see that the religious life of a nation on its intellectual side changes, not only because of the growth of language, but because of the positive additions to knowledge slowly gathered, which enable us to place the doctrines of the faith in truer mutual relations, which compel us to re-interpret the revelation we have received in terms of our own needs. Nothing short of this will justify what we call a liberal education ; nothing less can give us courage to investigate the truth in science and in history without any backward glance at the supposed results of our conclusions upon our received theology. And—most important of all—no other conception of religious life is so profoundly Christian; for it emphasizes our absolute trust in Him who is the Truth, and our abiding belief in the work of the Holy Ghost in earnest hearts, guiding them into all the truth.

And so, when we pray for the heavenly gift of the Comforter for the Church of Christ, we are not asking for any new or unfamiliar gift of which we have no experience. We pray that the guiding of a Father's counsel may be with us in the struggles, intellectual as well as practical, which beset and perplex our generation, being fully persuaded that as we have heard with our ears and as our fathers have told us the noble works which God did in their days and in the old time before them, so He will continue the like blessings to us. The Holy Ghost, the Lord, the Lifegiver, will teach us all things, not in our time nor in that of our children, but in that day when we shall have attained to perfect manhood, "to the measure of the stature of the fulness of Christ."

THE TOUCHSTONE OF TRUTH.

"The Church of the living God, the pillar and ground of the truth."—1 Tim. iii. 15.

Preached before the University of Dublin,
Whitsun Day, 1890

THE TOUCHSTONE OF TRUTH.

WHEN speaking last Sunday of the promise of the Comforter to the Church of Christ, I tried to show that this promise of continual instruction furnishes us with large hopes for the future guidance of the faithful into all the truth. That spiritual life is a process of growth, and that the gift of the Holy Ghost was no temporary or transient blessing, but that it is at once the source and the pledge of the vitality of the Church's message; this we saw was suggested by revelation and confirmed by history. But a very serious question will here present itself. If the Catholic faith thus exhibits traces of development in the course of centuries, if there is evidence that it has been filled with a larger meaning than was apparent in apostolic days, what reason have we for regarding it in its present form as in any degree final? How can we speak of it as absolutely true? May it not be that succeeding generations will see that our interpretations of Holy Scripture are as strained and unnatural as those of the Epistle of Barnabas or of Origen appear to us to be? Will not fresh developments present themselves in future? And with what right does Christianity, under these circumstances, claim to be the final and the perfect revelation of God's will to men? When the growth of spiritual life in the Church is described, is this meant to imply that Christianity too is destined to play its part on the theatre of the world, as preceding religions did, and then to depart from the stage with an approving and patronising *plaudite?*

Now, it is plain at the outset that so extreme a conclusion does not follow from the principle that spiritual life implies growth. The sum total of religious beliefs held at any one time is made up of permanent as well as of variable elements, and the change in the latter does not necessitate any change in the former. Christianity as a historical religion rests upon facts which do not change, though different aspects of the faith may come more or less into prominence at different periods. But we may fairly be challenged to point out where the permanent elements of Christianity are to be sought, and to consider whether and why there is any more hopeful prospect of right development in the thought of the Church than in the thought of the non-Christian world.

First, then, as to the special privilege of the Church to which our thoughts turn at Whitsuntide. We believe, indeed, that God overrules the affairs of all men, and we thankfully acknowledge that He has never left Himself without a witness among them; though there be fluctuations of greater or less magnitude, there is yet a low-water mark below which the tide of the eternal ocean of God's grace never falls. But our Lord spoke of the promise of the Comforter to His Church as if it were a new and a unique protection against error; and the Church of Christ has always believed that there are in her keeping special safeguards against mistake in things pertaining to God and to the destinies of the human soul. "He shall teach you all things"; "He shall take of mine and shall show them unto you"; "He shall guide you into all the truth";* these and the like utterances constitute a pledge that the Spirit of God will co-operate in the gradual education of Christendom in a peculiar sense. The real difficulty, however, is not the admission of this principle, which every Christian accepts, but the application of it to details. It has been granted that the divine leading does not guarantee freedom from error: where then does the especial privilege of the Church over the world manifest itself? It cannot be apparent in

* St. John xiv. 26; xvi. 13, 14.

individuals; we make no question indeed that the Holy Spirit acts on the minds of men who seek His guidance, but yet from the different conclusions at which they arrive in religious matters, we see that their individual peculiarities of temper and training are largely responsible for the beliefs they adopt.

No! if there be any touchstone of truth possessed by the Church of which the world knows nothing, we must look for it rather in the faith of the corporate society than in the faith of individuals; even in political and social questions we determine the central doctrine of a party by considering only that to which the party as a whole is committed. We have no right to make a great system responsible for the extravagance of individual supporters. And so this touchstone of truth must lie either in the truths which all Christians as a matter of fact hold in common and have always held, or in those doctrines to which Christendom is authoritatively committed by conciliar decrees. We need not here stop to consider the claims for a monopoly of truth put forward by the Bishop of Rome. Now, when we view the matter thus we see that there is at least one doctrine on which it can be said that all Christians are agreed, and it happens also to be one of the very few for which we have the officially declared consent of a united Christendom. The doctrine is that of our

Lord's incarnation. Christians differ among themselves much and bitterly about many things, but they all hold fast by this that the Founder of Christianity was the Christ, the Son of God. That God became man is *the* fact from which all Christian theology starts. The different inferences that have been drawn from that mystery illustrate the variety of the temperaments of mankind. But the fact itself is held by all those who have a right to the Christian name.

And again, for this doctrine we have the authoritative seal of a united Christendom. Before the schism which rent the East from the West, the Christian Councils had placed on record the doctrine of the Incarnation as constituting the rationale of the Church's existence. I do not speak now of the particular kind of authority which these Councils may enjoy: I only say that whatever degree of weight the venerable decrees of a General Council should have for us, that degree of weight attaches to the doctrine of the Incarnation as formulated at Nice and Chalcedon.

If we are asked, then, Is there any rock on which we may plant our feet in the midst of this stream of change which is carrying us along on its bosom? Is there any guiding star by whose light we may shape our course in life's journey? it will appear that there is one belief which is so much part and parcel of the Christian position that its mutilation or neglect would mean the death of Christianity. Christian men have differed about grace, free will, the sacraments, the mystery of the Atonement; but where there has been controversy about this, there has been apostasy from the Catholic faith. The Incarnation has always been regarded as at once the centre of the individual's faith and the justification of the Church's corporate life. Inferences from this great fact have, no doubt, been drawn out in many different directions; it is in this process of continual inference that the growth of intellectual life in the Church displays itself; but the fact itself at the basis of our speculations remains one and unchangeable. Here is a principle, belief in which is more than the assent to a dead tradition; it is a spring of living refreshment. Let us observe how it holds up to us a standard of truth and at the same time illustrates the degree of finality to which we may expect to attain.

It is plain that in their search after infallibility what men desire is that something shall be revealed to them so certainly and so distinctly that its expression can never change, and that there shall be no possibility of mistakes in drawing inferences from it. Nothing less than this seems satisfactory; and to certain minds the difficulty and the responsibility of right judgment appear so overwhelming that they will submit themselves to tradition, whether Protestant or Roman Catholic, to a party, to a pope, to anything with the semblance of authority, from sheer dislike of effort. They sacrifice their birthright of freedom in the vain attempt to rid themselves of individual responsibility. Now God has never revealed truth to men in such a way that they could not reject it if they would—in such a way that it cannot be mistaken. God gives us opportunities for arriving at truth; He never forces us to take advantage of them. His gifts are always tempered by the medium through which they are transmitted. Take an example, the gift of Holy Scripture. It is surely none the less the revelation of God's will because it betrays the presence of human agency on every page. It is a historical growth bound up with the national life of a great people, but it is none the less for that in a very real sense a *revelation*. The sacredness of Scripture is an entirely different thing from the verbal inerrancy of Scripture, just as the holiness of the Church as the sphere of the Holy Spirit's activity is a very different thing from its infallibility. Now the central fact on which Christianity rests, which is the heart of the Christian revelation, the fact that God became man, is a fact which contains in itself, if we will but see it, this very lesson that in God's highest gifts there is a union of the finite and infinite, of the changeful and the eternal. That the lesson is needed we shall see if we consider on what grounds the infallibility of the Church has been defended. Are they not briefly these? The Church of Christ has God's blessing; the promise of the Comforter, of which we read on Whitsunday, is a promise which seems to say to us that the true mind of the Church, the Body of Christ, is the mind of the Spirit of Christ. The Head of the Church is Christ; is she not then infallible? But apart from the practical difficulty of finding the organ through which the infallible decrees of the Church are to be transmitted to men, there is a further consideration which should guard us from hasty inference. Our blessed Lord, the Head of the Church, was indeed very God, but He was very man as well. Is there any one of us who is prepared to state exactly what that involves? We cannot forget that in His divine condescension He "emptied Himself,"* and that He "increased in wisdom and stature, and in favour with God and man."†

How far, or whether at all, the assumption of human nature by the Son of God was accompanied by or involved a voluntary limitation of the omniscience,

* Phil. ii. 8. † St. Luke ii. 52.

the omnipresence, the omnipotence of the Godhead, is a question from which reverent contemplation will shrink; but surely it is a question which, if put to us, we could not answer with complete confidence. It has appeared to many that the perfect humanity of the Saviour implied that He should have emptied Himself of these attributes of Deity during His earthly ministry. It is not now suggested that this inference is just; we so little comprehend the mystery of the Incarnation that all such speculations must be more or less guess-work. But at least it is an inference which has been made by pious men, and the legitimacy of it cannot readily be disproved. And it well illustrates the unwisdom of dogmatic over-statement about the infallibility of the Church, as typified by our Lord's incarnation. If the Church's Master voluntarily emptied Himself of His omniscience in that miracle of divine mercy, surely it is too much to claim that the Church itself shall be unfettered by the limitations of human infirmity when pursuing the thorny path of theological inference. But as our Lord was none the less God that He was man too, so is the treasure of the Church yet divine, though it be hid in earthen vessels. The Church of the living God has no voice so authoritative, that it deprives us of our personal responsibility in forming a " right judgment in all things;"

but yet she is the "pillar and ground of the truth." She has a divine deposit to guard, and, under the guidance of a divine Comforter, a divine message to deliver; he will be bold indeed who will count her rule of faith antiquated or obsolete, because with fuller knowledge and larger experience she has been enabled to read with more clearness between the lines of her charter. It is entirely consonant with the conjunction of two natures, the human and the divine, in the person of our blessed Lord, that in the teaching of His Church that which is divine should be presented under forms of man's devising; and the analogy may suggest to us that the Church's increase in divine wisdom from age to age affords no reason for rejecting her claim to be in a special sense the custodian of the truth.

So then, in our search after an infallible standard of authority, we seem to come upon it at last in the doctrine of the Incarnation. Here is a truth, we may say, which is not an inference, but the expression of a fact; here is a truth which never grows old, but teaches new lessons to each succeeding generation; here is a truth which Christian devotion has ever guarded with jealousy, and which Christian theology has embodied in the creed of the Catholic Church. And again, here is a truth which is more than the revelation of a fact; it is a revelation, so to speak, of the method of revelation. He who was the Truth was Man as well as God; in that most perfect manifestation of Deity the finite and infinite had a meeting point. "In Him dwelt all the fulness of the Godhead," but "in bodily wise."*

Here are many lessons for us peculiarly appropriate to Whitsuntide, when we count up the gifts which the Holy Spirit has given us and has yet in store.

It teaches us a lesson of *caution*. The Bible is a divine gift; but in the interpretation of the Bible we dare not assume that the written Word is free from the ordinary imperfections due to the employment of human instruments, when we know that the Incarnate Word subjected Himself to the bonds of human flesh.

It teaches us a lesson of *reverence*. As the errors and failures of the Christian Church present themselves to our gaze, we shall be slow to pass a cynical judgment of wholesale condemnation if we remember that when Almighty God revealed Himself most perfectly to men, it was not in the majesty of His glory, but in suffering and shame. It is of the Son of God that it was written, "There is no beauty in Him that we should desire Him."†

It gives us a message of *hope*. In the midst of

* Col. ii. 9. † Isaiah liii. 2.

that which is ever-changing, we have something on which to rest. We need not be troubled at the varying aspects which the faith of Christendom presents from generation to generation ; we need not fear that we are altogether the victims of the prejudices of our day, the slaves of the Time-spirit; for we know that in Christ we have the truth, and that the truth will make us free.

THE TEACHING OFFICE OF THE CHURCH.

"He gave some, apostles; and some, prophets; and some, evangelists; and some, pastors and teachers; for the perfecting of the saints, for the work of the ministry, for the edifying of the body of Christ: till we all come in the unity of the faith, and of the knowledge of the Son of God, unto a perfect man, unto the measure of the stature of the fulness of Christ; that we henceforth be no more children, tossed to and fro, and carried about with every wind of doctrine."—Eph. iv. 11-14.

Preached before the University of Dublin,
Sunday next before Advent, 1890.

THE TEACHING OFFICE OF THE CHURCH.

WE have presented to us, in a simple and striking manner, on this the last Sunday in the ecclesiastical year, the functions and claims of the Church. For, as we have got to the end of the table of proper lessons, and to the last of the Collects, Epistles, and Gospels, and are going to begin again next Sunday, we are reminded that there is a certain body of doctrine which the Church regards as essential to our spiritual welfare. The portions of Holy Scripture upon which our meditation is fixed from Sunday to Sunday, are not selected by the arbitrary caprice of the minister or the wishes of his congregation, but are appointed by the Church. And the words of St. Paul which I have just read seem to supply us with that view of the office of the Church as a teacher, which thus naturally comes under our notice to-day. Our Lord, we are told, "appointed some, apostles; some, prophets; . . . some, pastors and teachers . . . that we henceforth be no more children, carried about with every wind of doctrine."

Now here is presented to us a function of the Church which demands our most serious consideration at the present time, when those are not wanting who tell us that her message is incomplete, and that the revelation which she professes to give us is but one among many revelations to which men have given credence. Some go much further than this, and assure us that far from being final, her formulæ are not even true, but are obsolete and unmeaning. Christianity, in fact (for this is what is often meant though it is not openly expressed), is but a transitory phase of religious thought. It has done some good, say these friendly and patronising critics; but it is out of date. The apostles are not to be our teachers, for we are far wiser than they. The new wine of science has burst the old bottles into which it has been poured by the pious children of the Church.

When, however, we ask for some reasons in support of this grave indictment, we receive an answer which is simply astounding from its splendid audacity. We are told (what everyone who has thought upon the matter knows and will admit) that the increase of knowledge has made it necessary for Christian men to restate their beliefs as to many matters of religious interest. We do not think now, as John Wesley thought, that a belief in witchcraft is bound up with belief in the Bible; we do not think either that the power of curing a particular form of disease is inherent by divine providence in the person of the Christian Kings of England. What, Churchmen say, indeed, is that such advance in knowledge of the secrets of nature and of God is exactly what we might expect if our Lord's promise of a Comforter who should guide the Church into all the truth were a reality, exactly what we might expect from the analogy of the older revelations of God which were made "at sundry times and in divers manners."* But we are told, on the other hand, that as we have found ourselves mistaken on some points, we cannot be sure about any; that the growth of religious knowledge from age to age implies its general untrustworthiness at any given age.

To this question we then address ourselves and we ask, in the first instance: Is it true that, in science generally, the increase of knowledge always tends to overthrow rather than to supplement the older generalisations? Does the adoption of wider views as to matters of detail, as to particulars, prove that the general principles upon which our reasoning has been governed in the past were altogether un-

* Heb. i. 1.

reliable? It surely proves nothing of the sort. The science of mathematics is advancing at the present day by leaps and bounds. The general conceptions which formerly guided us are seen to be inadequate for the requirements of modern analysis. But no one supposes therefore that the doctrines of Newton's "Principia" are untrue. They are quite true as far as they go. And this example might of itself teach us that the adoption of wider views and larger ideas does not compel us to regard all our old conclusions as unsound.

We have taken an illustration from the field of pure science; let us borrow another from the domain of ethics. A difficulty very similar to that under consideration meets us when we attempt to investigate the nature of conscience. On the one hand the authority of its voice seems to assign to it an origin other than of earth; it is "the voice of God speaking in us." And yet, on the other hand, it seems tolerably certain that our conscience is an evolved product, analogous in the history of its growth to our arms or our legs. We can see the process of development going on before our eyes. In the civilised and Christian nations of Europe the development has reached a high level; in the savage of Central Africa it is only beginning. The dictates of the conscience of the child races of the world are far inferior, in point of an ideal morality, to the voice of modern Christendom. Are we then to assume, because the moral sentiments of mankind vary from age to age, from nation to nation, that there is nothing right or wrong in itself, but that all actions, high-minded and mean, cruel and kindly, are alike *natural;* and that it only depends upon circumstances whether they are judged good or evil? Surely we are saved from such a conclusion by remembering that conscience is a complex product, not a simple faculty; it is made up of two widely dissimilar factors—one divine, rational, moral, telling us that there is such a thing as the Good and the True to be followed at all hazard; the other human, empirical, social, offering suggestions as to what the right or wrong in any given case may be. The latter varies with circumstances, not so the former. The variation of a product is quite consistent with the permanence and constancy of one of the factors of which it is composed. And the modification of our moral verdicts by the friction of society and custom does not at all disprove the claim made for conscience by the believer in God, that it has the authority of Him in whose image we are made.

Now the principle to which we have here appealed will enable us to explain the contradiction which, it is said, emerges when we contrast the vacillations of the Church's teaching in matters of detail with the claim for supernatural guidance which she has always made. As conscience does, she claims a divine authority; as in the case of conscience this claim is met by the alleged imperfection and incompleteness of her message at any given epoch. If there is no real contradiction in the one case, it may be fairly urged that neither is there any such in the other.

It will be said, however: All this is possible in theory; but as a matter of practice, how do you propose to determine the permanent elements in the faith of the Church? Such there may be, no doubt; but if they are so mixed up with the transitory and imperfect, it may be past human ingenuity to find any safe criterion by which the divine may be separated from the human, the true from the false.

A fair challenge, and one which we are bound to meet. And it is not a practical answer to say —what is of course true—that these permanent elements of Christianity are to be found in Holy Scripture; for men's interpretations of those sacred volumes differ so widely, that if the Bible were taken to be the *immediate* standard by which each man were to try the truth, Christianity would cease to be an objective or universal religion at all. It would vary according to the whims and the prejudices of the individual interpreter. To use the old illustration, in which there is a great deal of good sense, the Bible so regarded is like a nose of wax, which each man can twist into the shape that best pleases him.

But, putting aside this rough-and-ready solution, let us ask ourselves how we would answer our parallel question in the region of morals? Are there any permanent elements in the morality of mankind? Conscience has erred in the past just as surely as the Church has erred. Are its dictates then all alike untrustworthy? Is its voice to be disregarded? Is this indeed the miserable result of that long process of education by which God has been training men to look beyond nature and sense? Is the development of conscience so blind and without purpose that its laws are nothing better than the transitory expedients of the moment? Few will dare to give such an answer as this. Just because the evolution of our moral faculty is the growth of an organic germ and not blind drifting, the moral laws which a man or a race adopts after the hard discipline of life are indeed the most trustworthy of all the laws by which human conduct is governed. Justice, truth, charity, these are the laws to which the development of conscience leads; and they are distinguished from mere social rules by an unmistakable and remarkable criterion. No race which has once learnt them ever professedly denies their authority: there is no retrogression in this development. The permanent elements of morality are to be sought in those moral laws which once apprehended are never again consciously rejected. That is the only working criterion which can be given. The extravagances of custom and the vagaries of fashion from time to time impose rules upon the conscience of a race which it rejects as soon as it has attained to that fuller light which comes with age. But the eternal laws of good and evil are never abandoned once they have been received.

And when we come to inspect the charter of that divine society which is one day to embrace the whole human race, the Christian Church, we find that the permanent principles which underlie her life can be distinguished from the transitory regulations which have been imposed upon her, or which she has imposed upon herself, in a somewhat similar fashion. The voice of the Church has sometimes—often, if you will—been misleading, and she has corrected her mistakes with advancing intelligence. But there are certain principles so essential to her life that the renunciation of them, or mistake about them, would mean her death. These cannot pass away. God's guidance of the Church as of the world is a phrase which has a real meaning. The growth of religious thought is not blind; it is the unfolding of the purpose of the ages. To the godless observer the wanderings of the Hebrews in the desert for those forty years of weariness must have seemed idle and to no end; but yet all the time an almighty Father was guiding them to the land of promise, so training them that though they should never enter it themselves, they should be able to recognise it, and greet it from afar. And when men tell us that the wanderings of the Church are aimless, that her mistakes are manifold, that she will never reach the end of her journey, for in truth there is no definite goal upon which her eyes are fixed, we shall reply that we are content to advance step by step, following the Light which leads through the darkness, refreshed by the stream that flows from the Rock.

A mere metaphor! it will be said. Metaphor is not argument. Tell us where are the permanent elements of Christianity. What truths are there about which there has been no mistake?

Well, then, if I have brought you with me so far; if I have shown you that the highest laws of morality are only attained through many failures; that God's way of dealing with men is not miraculously to prevent them from ever making mistakes about Him; that the test by which we always separate the result of genuine development from the unmeaning drift of fashion, is the practical one of universal consent, long continued and never reversed, then you must admit further that there is nothing unreasonable in the claim of the Catholic Church that she has permanent elements of truth enshrined in her creeds.

Men speak of the vagaries of Christian teachers, of the vacillating attitude of Christendom towards many great problems; but there is one circumstance they are very apt to overlook, which is much more striking than any change that has taken place; and that is the absolute fixity with which the Catholic Church has held to the Nicene Creed as the best expression of the truth which she has been able to formulate. Do I say it is the final expression of the truth? Certainly not; no man dare say that anything expressed in human language is final, in the sense that a larger statement may not be hereafter found which will embrace it. But it would be a singular inconsequence to conclude that therefore it is not true. Its propositions satisfy the same kind of test as the moral laws, which are universally recognised as binding on humanity. Within the circle of the Church the creeds have never been repudiated, as the moral laws have never been rejected, once received. And so, when people tell us that the Church does not know her own mind, that as she grows in wisdom and knowledge she is ever contradicting her past teaching, that she has proved her own incapacity as a teacher by her vacillations, we may meet such a statement by a simple denial.

There has never been any reversal of the dogmas contained in the creeds; they are still what they ever were to the sons of the Church. It is not indeed suggested that this universal consent is what gives them their ultimate authority; I have not entered into that question at all. It is too serious a question to discuss briefly at the end of a sermon. But this Catholic consent furnishes a complete answer to the charge of inconsistency brought against Catholic doctrine. The moral government of God, the incarnation and the atonement of our blessed Lord, the guidance of the Comforter, the future life of the soul, the divine society on earth and in heaven, these are the cardinal doctrines of Christianity. It is an absolute perversion of the facts to say that they have ever been denied by the Catholic Church. They have, as a matter of history, been held *semper, ubique, ab omnibus*, everywhere, always, and by all. These are the medicines unceasingly offered for the healing of the nations.

So, while thankfully recognising that the Holy Spirit is ever leading the Church into fuller knowledge, let us beware of that idolatry of change and that complacent self-laudation which are such conspicuous features of our own time. We are " the heirs of all the ages." True, but let us remember that if we are heirs we have an inheritance transmitted to us which it is our bounden duty to guard and to pass on unimpaired to those who shall come after us. " Keep that which is committed to thee," said St. Paul to Timothy, " and turn away from profane babblings."* You are not going to reject the eternal laws of justice, truth, charity, because conscience has often made mistakes; are you going to be so mad as to reject the highest truths about God which He has revealed to men through His Church merely because the Church has made mistakes? God forbid.

"Ask for the old paths, where is the good way,"† said the prophet. It is a narrow way indeed, and men have made it narrower by their own intolerance and presumption ; but it is lit by the light of heaven and it leads to the land of promise. Will you go out into the wilderness, or will you stay in this narrow path? It is not an easy path; it is full of difficulty, full of hazard, but before you as you journey is One who will be your stay in life and in death. "Follow me" is His invitation. And the hearts of all who have sought to follow that great Leader give the same response: "Lord, Thou hast been our refuge from one generation to another."

* 1 Tim. vi. 20. † Jer. vi. 16.

THE LETTER AND THE SPIRIT.

K

"The letter killeth, but the spirit giveth life."—2 Cor. iii. 6.

Preached before the University of Oxford,
Twenty-second Sunday after Trinity,
1893.

THE LETTER AND THE SPIRIT.

WHEN he wrote these words, St. Paul seems to have had in his mind the contrast between Judaism and Christianity. He rejoices that he no longer feels himself bound to preach the necessity of obeying all the minute precepts of the Mosaic law; he is a minister of "a new covenant," which counts singlemindedness and honesty of purpose as far more pleasing to God than an unceasing routine of petty observances. Obedience to the letter of the ceremonial law of the Hebrews is not required of a Christian man; in the liberty wherewith Christ has made him free, he is called to that higher and more difficult form of obedience which strives to enter into and fulfil the spirit of the divine commands. Judaism had then reached a period in its history when devotion to the letter of the principles upon which it was founded had ceased to be the spring of spiritual life. And the Apostle of the Gentiles, who saw that the law in the past had done its work of preparation for the Gospel, also saw that nothing short of a final rejection of its particular enactments could enable the new religion to make its way among "all sorts and conditions of men." We know how, in spite of opposition within the Church, St. Paul's view prevailed; we know how the recognition of the Christ as "the fulfiller of the law" was found to be quite consistent with the abandonment of its literal commands; and we thankfully acknowledge that the Church of Christ, in casting away the bondage of the ceremonial law, was able to retain for herself all that was noblest and most spiritual in the teaching of the psalmists and prophets of Israel. The rejection of the letter did not involve the loss of that spiritual inheritance to which the faithful are entitled as the true children of Abraham.

The principle asserted in the text applies with justice to many topics not immediately present to St. Paul's mind. All the words of genius admit of manifold application far different from the intention of him who first used them; and in even a deeper sense is this true of the words of Holy Scripture. They apply with as much freshness to the circumstances of to-day, as if they had been recorded and transmitted for the sole instruction of our generation. There is a catholicity, a wideness of range, in the language of the New Testament writers which impresses us the more, the more familiar we become with their words. And we shall thus not be untrue to the teaching of St. Paul if we try to see how the principle of our text holds good in directions other than those thought of by him. "The letter killeth, but the spirit giveth life." The order of religious development is from the straitness of the letter to the freedom of the spirit. There always comes a stage when blind obedience to rules will fail to satisfy; when the demand for principles becomes imperative.

This we all recognise in the teaching of children. We give children simple rules of conduct for guidance, and, so long as they are children, their consciences will approve them if they obey, will reprove them if they disobey the commands imposed. But when they grow a little older they begin to ask for reasons. They want to know why the rule is laid down at all, what is really gained by enforcing it, what ill effects to themselves or to anyone else would follow from disobedience. And then we have to give them principles; we explain to them that, as they are approaching an age of responsibility, they must not think so much of the letter of the rules which guided them when children, as of the spirit which they were intended to express. They may now "put away childish things." And, as we all know very well, the attempt to enforce rigid rules, upon those who have arrived at an age to understand and appreciate principles, not infrequently ends in disaster. There is a certain stage at which we must pass from the narrowness of the letter to the freedom of the spirit.

And, among children of a larger growth, we think far more highly of a man who uses the reason that God has given him to determine the right course at a perplexing crisis, than of one who governs his life by rules of casuistry. True, it is better to be the slave of logic than to be the slave of passion. It does not need a preacher to tell us that. But the slavery of logic is a real bondage; the cruel, the unrighteous, the foolish course is sometimes taken by a man just because he is afraid to trust his own judgment, and prefers to shift the responsibility of decision from himself to his principles. Often, indeed, does it happen that the letter kills, while the spirit quickens.

This is not only true of individual life; it is true of national life. In the beginnings of the constitution, the law enacted by Parliament was the only safeguard that was deemed necessary for the well-being of society; and at first the administration of the Court of King's Bench was sufficient for the needs of the nation. But as time went on, and as the fabric of society grew more complex, it was seen that injustice was often done through a too strict adherence to the letter of the law. *Summum jus, summa injuria* has passed into a proverb. It at last became manifest that it would not be possible to lay down rules which should cover every contingency that might arise; and provision was gradually made for legal tribunals which should be guided by the principles of the constitution, rather than by stereotyped formulæ. The existence of our Courts of Equity is a standing witness to the recognition by the nation of the truth that "the letter killeth, but the spirit giveth life." Edmund Burke is reported to have said that "no man understands less of the majesty of the English Constitution than the *nisi prius* lawyer, who is always dealing with the technicalities of precedence." We may or may not accept this severe judgment of a great statesman; but, at all events, it is abundantly plain that as the Courts of Equity have grown, the majesty of the law has been in no way impaired; rather have its declarations been received with a larger confidence. Thus as the stream of the national life has grown deeper and wider, its direction has been from the iron-bound fastness of literal enactment towards the free ocean of righteousness and charity. The tendency in the discipline of a nation, as in the discipline of a child, is to advance from the letter to the spirit.

We may trace something of the same law in the history of religion. In the period preceding that great religious revival which we call the Reformation, there were not wanting indications that punctilious obedience to the rules laid down by the Church was failing to promote true spiritual life. The traffic in indulgences and the abuse of penance were but the outcome of that spirit which would measure the morality of conduct by its conformity to certain prescribed maxims of casuistry. To many of these maxims in themselves there is no serious objection : they were the result of the multiplied experience of men meditating upon the perplexities of life, and wishing to determine once for all what the right course was in all possible cases. But once it was rediscovered that true religion does not consist so much in a man's outward acts as in the spirit in which he does them, a natural reaction set in, and the whole edifice of casuistry, with its superstructure of penances and indulgences, received a shock from which it has not yet recovered. The great importance attached by the Reformers to faith as contrasted with works is only fully explicable when we consider it in this light. Men saw that " the letter killeth."

In a speculative point of view the problem assumed a somewhat different aspect, and the whole question seemed to turn on the authority of the

Church. If the Church was indeed the abode of the Spirit of Christ, it was asked, how could she have been mistaken in her dealing with souls in the past; nay, how could she ever be mistaken at all? We can hardly understand, in our altered circumstances, how terrible must have been the shock to devout men and women to find that the teaching of the Church was no longer considered infallible by those to whom they looked as their spiritual masters. "General Councils," says our 21st Article, "may err and sometimes have erred in things pertaining unto God." Why, if that be so, what is the guarantee of religious truth? Is not the Church's authority absolutely bound up with her infallibility? We can readily see now that authority and infallibility are two very different things, and we thankfully recognise and gladly defer to the authority of the Catholic Church on the main issues of the Catholic faith, without feeling ourselves to be disloyal to the 21st Article. The Church may err in particular decisions, but we see that the whole drift and course of her teaching has been towards righteousness, that she is, despite failure and sin, the custodian of the truth as she is the home of grace. We recognise the presence of the divine Spirit in her life, while we do not consider ourselves bound by the letter of all her occasional enactments. The alarm, then, that was felt at the time of the Reformation, was unreasonable; it was based on a misapprehension; the authority of the Church is not destroyed, though we now understand better what it means. The drift has been again from "the letter to the spirit." Such a lesson as this could not be learnt without much heart-searching; nay, is it certain that we have learnt the true lesson of the Reformation yet? What is the most prominent religious question of our own day? I suppose it is the question as to the authority of Holy Scripture. Let us consider how St. Paul's words apply to it.

When the Reformers declared that the guidance of the Church, though valuable and not to be lightly discarded, did not guarantee the infallibility of her teaching, men began to cast about for some other source of authority which might be to them what the Church had been in the past. From the principle that Holy Scripture was the supreme authority in matters of faith and morals, the transition was easy to the assumption that its language in every syllable must be infallibly exact. And this served for a time, as long as the human conscience was not allowed to judge of its moral teaching, or the human intellect to weigh its scientific and historical statements. But, first, as regards its moral teaching, men gradually began to see that to give up one's conscience to the teaching of the Bible was the same kind of mistake as to give it up to the teaching of the Church, and that the results of forbidding conscience to have a voice in matters relating to the life of the soul were likely to prove disastrous. Butler, with that profound common-sense which constitutes not the least of his claims on our attention, declared that reason must be regarded as having a right to judge of revelation. He emphasized the great principle that nothing, neither Church nor book, neither the divine society nor the divine word, must come between the individual soul and God. Butler wrote one hundred and fifty years ago, and the far-reaching significance of his words has hardly, as yet, received full attention. But once the point had been raised, it became plain to all who allowed themselves to think upon the matter, that there was a steady growth of moral ideas all through the Bible, that the morality of the Old Testament was not the morality of the New Testament, the teaching of the law not on the same lofty level as the sublime words of the prophets. And now the rights of conscience have been vindicated, and there is a general willingness to allow that in this matter we must not look to the letter of a special saying, a special psalm, but to the spirit and tendency of the whole dispensation. Butler dwelt indeed on the morality of particular precepts recorded in the Old Testament, and was at pains to justify it; but it is in large measure due to Butler himself that we have learnt that it is by the spirit which pervades the entire literature that we ought to judge it.

Once more. The question is often asked—we are asking it, I doubt not, of ourselves. Does our acceptance of the Old Testament as a divine first-lesson book require us to believe that the most minute details of the history are recorded with infallible accuracy? Is it essential to our belief in the inspiration of Holy Scripture that we should hold it impossible that the writers of the various books could have made any mistakes as to scientific or historical fact? Is the authority of the Bible, as a guide, bound up with the belief that there can be no discrepancies between the parallel narratives of the same event to be found in its pages? Are these questions really foreclosed for a Christian man? Some tell us that they are, and prophets are not wanting who warn us that the authority of Scripture as a practical guide to life, and belief in the inspiration of its authors by the divine Spirit, absolutely depend on acceptance of its verbal infallibility. They declare that we cannot preserve the spirit unless we preserve the letter.

Now whatever be the truth as to the alleged

errors of fact in the Old Testament, it is to be observed that predictions of this sort are worth very little as argument. Similar predictions were, no doubt, made by his friends as to the consequences that would inevitably result from St. Paul's new doctrine that the Mosaic law was not binding on Gentile converts. We can well imagine how plausibly it could have been maintained that St. Paul had renounced his allegiance to the Jewish Scriptures; and how difficult it must have been to appreciate the sincerity of his words when asking, "Do we then make void the law through faith?" he boldly answered, "God forbid: yea, we establish the law."*
St. Paul was a brave man. He looked facts in the face. We shall do well to follow his example.

It would be alike unprofitable and unwise to dwell upon the trifling discrepancies that have been detected between various statements of the Old Testament. They are (as has been well said) but like spots on the sun which do not diminish its glory or its usefulness to any appreciable extent. It would be sheer waste of opportunity to spend time upon them. But it is of the last importance to observe that we have no warrant, either in Scripture or in reason, or in the declarations of the Christian Church, for declaring that they cannot exist in an inspired

* Rom. iii. 31.

literature. The more completely we grasp that the substantial truth of a record is not affected by passing and petty inaccuracies, that inspiration does not necessarily involve either infallibility or verbal inerrancy, the more shall we enter into the meaning of St. Paul's profound words, " the letter killeth, but the spirit giveth life." Scripture—we may be sure of it —will thus lose none of its authority. The authority of our human teachers does not lose its force when we learn that they are not possessed of encyclopædic knowledge, and that they may occasionally make mistakes in matters which lie outside their proper province. Once that stage in our education has been reached, we gratefully recognise how valuable their teaching has been. They have taught us, while deferring to them, to think for ourselves. So is it with the Church. So is it with Holy Scripture. The Bible is our teacher still, nay, more than ever our teacher; it has taught us, and yet teaches us, to think.

We have seen that even in the ordinary matters of life, the transition from the letter to the spirit is a transition which daily comes under our observation, and, further, that it is attended by no ill results either in theory or in practice. This is true, I have said, even in the commonplace routine of life, in the education of children, as in the growth of a nation. And it is not unreasonable to suppose that, as He who is the Light of the world is also the Lord of the Church, a similar progress may be anticipated in the province of religion. But the truth is, that when we come to inspect the problems of revelation, we see that there is even a deeper reason why the same law should hold good here. Were the principles involved in the statements of Scripture like the principles, let us say, of an ordinary political party, such as can be precisely expressed in the form of a speech from the throne, then we might expect (though, perhaps, not with entire confidence) that they would be simple to understand and easy to apply in practice to every case that could arise. The meaning of an Act of Parliament is, we are often told, what it says. There is no appeal from the letter to the spirit in the interpretation of it. It has no conscience, it has no soul. But surely we are on different ground when we are dealing with the record of a revelation from God to man. From the nature of the case, such a revelation cannot be reduced to precise formulæ, easy to apply and obvious to interpret. It is apparent, at the outset, that it may be expected to involve more than can ever be expressed in words. The more we reflect on the condescension implied in such a communication of the infinite Creator with His creation, the more we feel that human language is but an imperfect vehicle for the transmission of the divine voice. And when we say that Christendom, in the interpretation of Holy Scripture, has learnt in part, and is still learning, how to pass from the straitness of the letter to the freedom of the spirit, what is this but to say that the Church of Christ attains daily to a better understanding of the revelation she has received?

It will be urged, perhaps, that however attractive such a theory of Christian progress may appear, yet it will be found impossible to apply it in practice without disaster. For that in the first place it suggests that there is no finality in any results at which we have arrived in the past, or may arrive in the future; and that, in the second place, it supplies us with no plain and unmistakable guide to conduct such as men naturally desire.

It would be impossible to enter here upon so large and momentous a question as the permanence of the Christian creeds; but it is not difficult to see that the question does not necessarily arise out of what has been said. To hold that in the discipline of a nation, of a Church, of a soul, a larger and more gracious significance is ever being found in the moral and spiritual revelation which God has given us of Himself, in no way forces us to the conclusion that our former interpretations of it were erroneous. Imperfect they may be, but not necessarily erroneous. In morals, and in religion, as in science, the increase of knowledge tends rather to supplement than to overthrow the older generalisations. The adoption of wider views as to matters of detail, as to parts, does not by any means show that the general principles upon which our reasoning has been governed in the past are altogether unreliable.*

Take an illustration somewhat nearly related to our subject. In the development of that moral sense which is one of God's most certain and most precious gifts to mankind, we can observe, as it seems, the operation of that law of progress of which we have been speaking. For consider in what does moral progress consist, either for an individual or a nation? Not surely in the discovery of new moral principles, but in the better appreciation of the meaning of those with which we are already familiar. " Thou shalt not kill;" here is a moral precept of which the moral basis is the recognition of the sacredness of human life and the dignity of the human person. And yet, not only in its original form as given to the Hebrews, but as expanded by the conscience of modern Christendom under the guidance of the spirit of Christ, it is believed by all but an insignificant section of *doctrinaires* to be quite consistent with the

* See p. 135 *supra*.

authorisation of capital punishment by the State, or with the unauthorised measures found needful in barbarous or half-civilised countries for the protection of the individual and the home. "Thou shalt not kill." Yes, that is the letter of the law. But the more completely a man enters into the spirit of the principle upon which it is based, the principle, as has been said, of the sacredness of human life, the more will he feel the imperative necessity of occasional violations of the letter.

And concurrently with this growing feeling that it is a righteous thing in certain obvious cases to disobey the letter, there arises a larger appreciation of the spirit. "Thou shalt not kill" comes to this, "Thou shalt not hate." He from whom the law proceeds, He of whose moral judgments our best thoughts as to right and wrong are but a feeble reflex, He is a God whose name is Love, His laws are laws of love. When occupied with such a precept as this, it is probably unnecessary to add that in the overwhelming majority of cases the righteous course is to abide by the letter of the law; it furnishes, for most of us in ordinary life, a quite sufficient guide. But the point upon which we may lay emphasis is this: No one will deny that the world has grown more jealous of the prerogatives of the individual man as the centuries have rolled by, that his life is regarded as a more precious thing than it was in the days of the Roman Republic, or, to go farther back, in the days of the patriarchs. The offer of Reuben to his father of his sons' lives if he failed to restore to him his Benjamin, is an offer which would be regarded as quite unjustifiable in a modern police-court. A father cannot thus, with impunity, barter away the lives of his innocent children. But while we recognise more fully the depth and the permanence of the moral principle underlying the commandment, "Thou shalt not kill," we find ourselves forced in the same breath to admit that occasional violations of the literal precept may, in conceivable cases, be demanded by a sensitive conscience. In the course of our moral education, as we pass from the bondage of the letter to the freedom of the spirit, we learn that it is not the old principle which was erroneous, but our imperfect interpretation of it. And the remarkable feature in the moral progress of nations, as far as it can be traced in the pages of history, is this, that no great moral principle once consciously received is ever openly repudiated. Justice, truth, charity, these are principles which are never abandoned once they have been received. And thus it becomes apparent that despite the changed aspect which, it is true, certain moral problems present from age to age, yet there is a sense in which it may be said that the solution offered at any given epoch is final. It is accurate so far as it goes; it is imperfect, but it is true. And in the greatest moral crisis in all history, we find this law of moral development laid down by Him whose moral insight is recognised even by those who are so unhappy as to have persuaded themselves that He is less than the eternal Son of God. The Christ Himself did not come to destroy the law, but to fulfil. He has taught us, as no one else has taught us, that the true disciple of the law is he who strives to enter into and obey its spirit. When we are told, then, by prophets of evil that the results of applying St. Paul's words in the text to the interpretation of Scripture will be fatal to a true reverence for Scripture itself, we may point with some confidence to the results of the application of the very same principles to the laws of individual morality. Their permanence, their sanctity, is not thus affected; nay, obedience to them rests on a firmer ground than before.

But if not in theory, yet in practice, it is urged that the difficulty of distinguishing between the letter and the spirit, of extracting the kernel from the husk, is so formidable that it may well deter prudent persons from the attempt. And though it be admitted that the task is one, properly speaking, for the Christian society at large, rather than for its individual members, yet even thus we do not save ourselves from perplexity. To steer a safe course over an angry sea needs far more skill in navigation than to ride peacefully at the old moorings; the beacon lights are hard to distinguish; we are liable to be misled by the lights displayed by our own comrades in this perilous venture.

All this is sadly true; and yet our only safety is found at times in leaving the harbour where we are slowly drifting towards the rocks and in boldly facing the gale. The ship of the Church of God has not been commissioned to rest securely in quiet waters, but to rescue those who are perishing without in the storm. Here is not our rest; that shall be gained when the voyage is over, when the Pilot in whom alone we put our trust shall have brought us to the haven where we would be.

THE INSPIRATION OF HOLY SCRIPTURE.

"It is written, that Abraham had two sons, the one by a bondmaid, the other by a freewoman. But he who was of the bondwoman was born after the flesh; but he of the freewoman was by promise. Which things are an allegory: for these are the two covenants."—Gal. iv. 22-24.

Preached before the University of Dublin,
Fourth Sunday in Lent, 1891.

THE INSPIRATION OF HOLY SCRIPTURE.

"WHICH things are an allegory." In this remarkable passage St. Paul lays down a principle in reference to the Scriptures of the Old Testament which enables us to see how high a place they occupied in the estimation of the early followers of Christ. He asserts that the story of Abraham's wives, and the record of the disputes in the patriarchal household, are not only interesting as history, but are allegorical of spiritual truth. And he elsewhere generalises and extends the principle here involved when he tells us that "Whatsoever things were written aforetime were written for our learning that we through patience and comfort of the Scriptures might have hope."* The history and literature of the Jews are regarded by him as possessing a more than local and transient importance; they are full of instruction for men of every race and of every generation.

* Rom. xv. 4.

In one sense, indeed, this allegorical application of history can be justified on general grounds without any appeal to the special prerogatives of Holy Scripture. History is always pregnant with principle; alike to him who does and to him who does not believe in revelation, the record of the past may be taken as the record of God's dealings with men in the course of His providence, and as suggestive therefore of counsel for their guidance in the future. And not only is it permissible to draw lessons from history; we may, and often do, derive from poem or romance principles of conduct of which the original writer never dreamed. It has always been recognised that teaching by parable is one of the most effectual methods of instruction. The use of a familiar illustration enables us to bring home to our hearers what we wish to impress upon their minds.

But St. Paul claims something more than this for the literature of the Old Testament when he says that " every Scripture inspired of God is profitable for teaching, for reproof, for correction, for instruction which is in righteousness."* In these and other passages he seems to speak of the Old Testament as containing God's message to men in a sense in which that message is not to be found in other books, *e.g.*, in the hymns of the Rig-Veda, or in the philosophy of

* 2 Tim iii 16.

Greece. And it is here that the difficulty as to the nature of the inspiration of Scripture emerges. The canonical books of the Old and New Testaments have been regarded for centuries throughout Christendom as *inspired* in some unique sense; but in what precisely that inspiration consists, how it manifests itself, what are its criteria, what its conditions, the Christian Church has never taken upon herself to say. Among a few small sects, no doubt, zeal for the authority of Scripture has outrun reverence for truth, and extravagant definitions of inspiration have been stereotyped. But no one of the great branches of the Catholic Church has been thus bold to define under what conditions this precious gift of God's word has been offered to men; it has been thankfully recognised that in the writings of the Old and New Testament God's word is *contained*, but it has been also felt that it was presented in "sundry portions and in divers fashions."

It has been a serious misfortune, a great danger to the Christian faith, that in this regard individuals and communities have been less cautious, less reverent, than the Church universal. It is not too much to say that the use made of the Bible even in our own country since the Reformation has been often marked by a superstition as gross as those others from which we were, in God's providence, rescued by the Reformation itself. Men—worthy men, Christian men—have not only persuaded themselves that every word (and apparently every word in the received translation) of those sacred volumes was directly dictated by the Spirit of God; but they have frequently used the Bible with as little intelligence as the poor pagan uses his fetish. This is not the place to speak of that irreverent indolence which would find out God's will, not by sober meditation, study, and prayer, but by opening the Bible at random and assuming that the first text on which our eye lights will, apart from its context, miraculously provide us with a guide to the present perplexities of life. We are little likely, in the intellectual atmosphere of a university, to fall into such extravagance as that; but it is well for us to remember what was the source of this theory of verbal inspiration which is now only a curiosity of exegesis. It arose, at least in part, from the natural indolence of human nature which looks about for an infallible guide in doctrine and in practice, that cannot be mistaken. The desire for such a guide is, indeed, entirely natural. As Bacon tells us, men love to have some Atlas or Pole on which they may rest their thoughts. It is a desire which has led men, before now, to submit themselves to the authority of the Pope of Rome. But it is none the less mistaken. God has not provided for us any such easy path to truth; Holy Scripture, divine gift though it surely be, is a gift for the full appreciation of which all the resources of human learning must be taxed; it is a gift to be used with discrimination as well as with thankfulness. And if we wish to find that blessing in its study, which God would have us find, we must be content to possess our souls in patience, to proceed by slow and cautious steps in our endeavour to determine in what its unique character consists—not assuming beforehand what inspiration *must* mean, but investigating with candour the phenomena which surround it. This will open a vast field of research, in which much yet remains to be done, and in which the workers are not yet agreed as to the methods of inquiry. It would be rash for any one (above all, for one not specially qualified) to speak with confidence as to the issue of the researches now being pursued as to the structure of the Old Testament. But it seems that even at this stage we may profitably remind ourselves that whatever be the nature of the inspiration of the Bible, it must be consistent with facts such as the following:

It must be consistent with the fact that some of the books are compiled from pre-existing materials. The Books of Chronicles are confessedly a compilation of this sort; the same is probably true of the Pentateuch, or, to go to the New Testament, of the

Synoptic Gospels. The inspiration, then, of a writer did not preclude him from using and incorporating in his work portions of older writings, for which no one claims inspiration in any special sense. It is in part (as has been well said) an inspiration of selection, rather than of composition.

In the second place, the Bible is the record of a revelation which was progressive; truth was revealed to men as they were able to bear it. And so in the earlier books we find sentiments expressed and deeds recorded without disapproval, which offend our moral instincts, and which we feel would certainly be wrong for us. Inspiration did not take the writers completely out of the moral conditions of their time; the men who were inspired to give God's message did not therefore rise to the level of the morality of Christendom. The inspiration, in short, of a special book, of a special psalm, is consistent with a moral tone which, however remarkable when the surroundings of the writer are taken into account, was yet imperfect.

And in the third place, though here, if anywhere, caution is needed, inspiration does not seem to have guaranteed historical or scientific accuracy in details. The Bible was certainly not meant to teach history or science, but to unfold the ways of God to man—so much we all believe; but it has been maintained that it is nevertheless impossible that any mistakes as to fact should occur in it. It has been assumed that the writers of the Bible were, one and all, so raised above the historical and scientific level of the age in which they lived, that every statement they make as to the origin of species or the history of Egypt or Assyria must be regarded as beyond criticism. And, no doubt, to anyone who believes in God such miraculous intervention is quite possible; the only question is, have we grounds for supposing it to have been exercised? Certainly the historians of the Bible make no such claim for themselves; and immunity from error, in matters not directly affecting the spiritual life and man's relation to his Maker, can only be claimed for them if it appears on the whole to be consonant with the facts. The question must be decided by an appeal, not to the prejudices of our own imagination, but to criticism which is honest as well as devout. Whichever way this question be settled, and it cannot be settled off-hand, the Christian faith remains unshaken. We believe in God, we accept with reverence the revelation of Himself given us in Holy Scripture, but we dare not say that its spiritual authority guarantees the complete historical accuracy of every passing remark of the sacred writers If we venture, on the other hand, to make Christianity answerable with its very life for the veracity of the minute details of the early Hebrew history, we are like children building upon the sand an edifice, which, however imposing to view, is liable at any moment to be swept away from before our eyes by the flowing tide of criticism.

"As incredible praises," says Hooker, "given unto men do often abate and impair the credit of their deserved commendation, so we must likewise take great heed lest in attributing unto Scripture more than it can have, the incredibility of that do cause even those things which indeed it hath most abundantly to be less reverently esteemed." *

In what candid sense, then, can we speak of the Bible as inspired? Or rather, what do we mean when we call it an inspired book? It might be said in the first place, that a religious man has a right to apply that term to any book which has led men to God. The Bible itself tells us that "Every good gift and every perfect gift is from above."† So we pray in the Collect that by the inspiration of God's Holy Spirit we ourselves may think those things that be good; or, again, that by the same inspiration the

* *Eccl. Pol.* II. viii. 7. See also Paley, *Evidences*, Part III., ch. 3. The subject is discussed with candour and reverence in Prof. Kirkpatrick's *Divine Library of the Old Testament* (1892), p. 103—7.
† James i. 17.

thoughts of our hearts may be cleansed. And thus, too, there is a sense in which a hymn like the *Te Deum* or—to go to a lower level—any great religious poem, may be spoken of without apparent unfitness as inspired. The influence of God's Spirit cannot be altogether absent from any writing in which men have found rest for their souls. But such considerations do not mark off the Bible as unique. Why do we regard it not only as God's gift, but as uniquely God's gift? And when we put the question thus we feel that, whatever other answers may be given, one reason is surely because the centre of the Bible is the person of our Lord Jesus Christ.

For the Christian, the New Testament containing the historical record of His deeds and words is inspired, for it recounts works such as none other man did; it records the words of Him who spake as man never yet spake, as well as the teaching of those apostles whom His Spirit was to guide into all the truth. And as regards the Old Testament, can we read it without feeling that Christ is its final cause? It is the overture to the Hymn of Redemption. It led up to that Redeemer who was to deliver the world from its sorrow and its sin. It guided pious hearts to expect a Messiah whose dominion should be world-wide, who was to partake of the divine nature, who was to receive gifts for men,

M

Imperfect as was the vehicle through which the divine message was delivered, yet the divine message was there. Not only in prophecy and psalm, but in the Law itself there are anticipations of the coming glory, of the advent of Him towards whom the whole creation moved. It is not hard to believe that a literature with such a consummation as this was produced under the divine guidance, and for the instruction of the Christian as well as of the Jewish Church. So St. Paul assures us that it was "written for our learning." And a greater than St. Paul. Our Lord told His disciples that of necessity all things "must be fulfilled which were written in the Law of Moses, and in the Prophets, and in the Psalms concerning Him"*; thus putting the seal of His authority on the principle that in law, prophecy, and psalm the divine counsels had been indicated to the world through the literature of the chosen race.

And thus the Church of Christ, following her Master's teaching, thankfully accepts Holy Scripture, believing that even as the divine Spirit guided the apostles, so too it was the Holy Ghost who spake by the prophets. The New Testament is the record of that for which the Old Testament was the preparation. Thus it is that the unique character of the Bible may, in part, be explained from the uniqueness

* St. Luke xxiv. 44.

of its subject. It deals with the person of Christ, who is the incarnation of God. And as in the Incarnate Word there were two natures, a divine and a human, so in the written word, with remarkable analogy, the divine and human elements are closely connected. We do not reject our Lord's Godhead because we believe Him to have been perfect man; and we do not at all depreciate the authority of the divine voice of Scripture if we listen too to those human voices of sadness, of joy, of despair and of triumph, which speak to our hearts from its pages.

One caution is, perhaps, not unneeded. Bishop Butler has remarked that it is one of the peculiar weaknesses of human nature, when, upon a comparison of two things, one has been treated as being of greater importance than the other, to regard this latter as of no importance at all.* And such a mistake is one to which the student of Scripture is specially liable. From the nature of the case critical studies are often directed rather to the analysis of the human element in the Bible than to the reception of that which in it is divine. But it would be a grievous mistake to suppose that any study of Holy Scripture could be of genuine profit which overlooked the fact that Scripture is the record of a revelation of God to man. The remembrance of this

* See *Analogy*, Part II., ch. i. *sub fin.*

will hallow our criticism, as it will moderate our confidence that we can fathom all the depths of its meaning.

And yet again. To use the Bible aright is not an end in itself, but a means. When Christian the Pilgrim was on his way to Mount Zion he did not tarry long in the house of the Interpreter. Many things he learnt there which helped him in the difficulties of his journey; but it was only a stage on his road. And so too for each of us there is a greater work prepared than even the study of the Bible, namely, the pressing forward in the Christian life; to this all means of grace, of which Scripture is one, are subordinate. But if we use the Bible with honesty, with patience, with prayer, we shall find its guidance as precious as did the pilgrim in Bunyan's story, for it will ever guide us in the way that leads to the City of God.

THE WORD OF GOD.

"And He said unto them, Full well ye reject the commandment of God that ye may keep your own tradition. For Moses said, Honour thy father and thy mother; and, Whoso curseth father or mother, let him die the death; but ye say, If a man shall say to his father or mother, It is Corban, that is to say, a gift, by whatsoever thou mightest be profited by me; he shall be free. And ye suffer him no more to do ought for his father or his mother; making the word of God of none effect through your tradition which ye have delivered; and many suchlike things do ye."—St. Mark vii. 9-13.

Preached before the University of Dublin
Sunday next before Advent, 1893.

THE WORD OF GOD.

THE meaning of the expression, "The word of God," which occurs so frequently in the pages of Scripture, has often been discussed. More especially the applicability of the phrase to the written record of revelation contained in the canonical books of the Old and New Testaments has been made the subject of debate. On the one hand, we find the Bible thus described, quite as a matter of course, in the popular religious phraseology of the day. And on the other hand, critics of eminence are not wanting who assure us that the phrase as used of Scripture is not justifiable by Scripture, and that its employment is to be deprecated as leading to false views about the authority of Holy Writ.

In the face of this conflict of opinion, it seems worth while to make an examination once again of the usage of the New Testament writers as to this striking and dignified expression. Such an examination can be neither simple nor easy, for many difficult questions of interpretation will present themselves as it proceeds, but it may be expected to prove instructive.

In the first place we observe that in a considerable number of passages the title, "The word of God," is applied to the incarnate Christ. We need not now inquire into the source of the phraseology employed by St. John in his Gospel and in the Apocalypse; whether the language used by him in unfolding his sublime teaching was suggested by the philosophy of Greece, or was due to Hebrew influence, is a large question which cannot here be discussed with the fulness that it requires. We are only concerned with the fact that, from whatever source the title was derived, it is applied by the apostle to our blessed Lord; and about this there is no doubt. "The Word was made flesh,"* he tells us in the prologue to his Gospel, and in the Apocalypse he writes of the righteous warrior whom he sees riding forth to judgment upon a white horse, "His name is called the Word of God."† And this (as it seems) is the usage not only of St. John but of other New Testament writers, as, *e.g.*, the author of the Epistle to the Hebrews.‡ Even outside the canonical books, in the writings of Philo the Jew, though here

* St. John i. 14.   † Rev. xix. 13.   ‡ Heb. iv. 12.

with hesitation and uncertainty, the phrase is similarly used of a great person who comprises in Himself the perfect revelation of God to men.

In a yet larger number of passages the expression may be taken in a wide sense as descriptive of the entire message of God to the world. It stands for the revelation itself, rather than for Him in whom the revelation centres. And the phrase ὁ λόγος τοῦ θεοῦ, taken thus, has an ambiguity or rather complexity of meaning in Greek which cannot be exactly reproduced in English. For it is implied that this utterance is not like the random and hasty speech of men; it is the manifestation of perfect intelligence, it is that eternal wisdom by which men shall best regulate their lives. It is hardly necessary to give instances of this, the commonest, sense in which the phrase under consideration is employed in Scripture. All through the book of the Acts of the Apostles the first preachers of Christianity are represented as promulgating the word of God, that is, the evangelical message with which they were entrusted. "It is not reason," they said, "that we should leave the word of God and serve tables."* "We are not," wrote St. Paul, in like manner in his second Corinthian letter, "as many, which corrupt the word of God."† The same apostle speaks to the Thessalonians of the

* Acts vi. 2. † 2 Cor. ii. 17.

responsibility which rested upon them, inasmuch as they had "received the word of God,"* *i.e.*, had heard the story of the Crucified from his lips. And he directs Titus to emphasize his exhortations to Christian wives, by reminding them that if they were guilty of any laxity in conduct "the word of God" would be "blasphemed," † *i.e.*, the Christian evangel would be evil spoken of. To turn to the Gospels, St. Luke speaks of the people who came in crowds to hear Jesus as having assembled "to hear the word of God;" ‡ and our Lord Himself described those who reverenced the divine message which He came to bring as "blessed," because having "heard the word of God" they "keep it." §

Thus it is apparent that "the word of God" often stands in the Christian Scriptures for the divine message revealed to men, indirectly by the prophets of the Old Testament and the apostles of the New Testament, and directly by Him whom prophets expected and apostles adored. This divine message is recorded, in part, in the pages of the Old Testament, and it is thus plain that in a certain sense the title, "the word of God," is applicable to the revelation of the divine counsels therein contained. The revelation recorded in the

* 1 Thess. ii. 13. † Titus ii. 5.
‡ St. Luke v. 1. § St. Luke xi. 28.

sacred literature of the Hebrews, would unquestionably have been regarded by a Jew as truly "the word of God." We may be sure that no apostle would have excluded Scripture from the agencies to which the title might be given. And if the question had been asked of an apostolic preacher, Where then is this λόγος θεοῦ of which you speak? from the evidence before us we can hardly doubt that he would have answered that, in whatever other ways and fashions it had been manifested, yet in the Hebrew Scriptures it was conspicuously present.

But we pass on from these general considerations, and we ask, Is there any passage in the New Testament in which the phrase under discussion not only *may* be applied, but *must* be applied, to the Scriptures of the elder dispensation, in which there is an exclusive reference to the written record of revelation rather than to the message orally delivered by preachers of righteousness speaking in the name of God? This is a question not altogether easy to answer with confidence; but it is worth while to note two passages, one in the Pauline Epistles, one in the Synoptic Gospels, in which such a limitation seems to be required by the context.

First, let us fix our attention on a sentence in which St. Paul, when writing to Timothy, sets forth the anti-Christian character of certain ascetic extravagances which he foresaw would soon become prominent in the Church. "In the latter times," he says, "some shall depart from the faith," giving heed to persons who bid them abstain from meats which God meant to be received with thankfulness. "For every creature of God is good, and nothing to be refused if it be received with thanksgiving: for it is sanctified by the word of God and prayer."* It is hard to understand this otherwise than by interpreting the word of God † here spoken of as referring to the Scriptural phraseology which entered largely into the grace before meat customary in pious households. The language of the Old Testament formed, we may well suppose, as large a portion of the prayers of religious men in the days of St. Paul, as the language of the New Testament does of our own liturgical forms of devotion; ‡ and it is thus not surprising to find the apostle speaking of meat which had been blessed by a petition breathing the language of Scripture as "sanctified by the word of God and prayer." To suppose that St. Paul intends nothing

* 1 Tim. iv. 3—5.
† The passage is thus taken by many good commentators, *e.g.*, by Bishop Ellicott, Alford, and B. Weiss.
‡ In the "Apostolic Constitutions," vii., 49, there stands the following grace before meat: εὐλογητὸς εἶ, κύριε, ὁ τρέφων με ἐκ νεοτητός μου, ὁ διδοὺς τροφὴν πάσῃ σαρκί. πλήρωσον χαρᾶς καὶ εὐφροσύνης τὰς καρδίας ἡμῶν, ἵνα πάντοτε πᾶσαν αὐτάρκειαν ἔχοντες, περισσεύωμεν εἰς πᾶν ἔργον ἀγαθὸν ἐν Χρ. Ἰησοῦ, τῷ κυρίῳ ἡμῶν, δι' οὗ σοὶ δόξα, τιμὴ καὶ κράτος εἰς τοὺς αἰῶνας. ἀμήν.

THE WORD OF GOD. 189

so definite as this, and that in this verse he means to convey nothing more than that the Gospel message has removed the restrictions of the Mosaic Law,* is to adopt methods of exegesis which would deprive, I do not say the New Testament, but all literature of any certain meaning.

Another interpretation has, however, been put upon this confessedly difficult passage, which demands a word in passing. It has been supposed that in it we have a reference to that sanctification of material things which seems to have been involved in the fact of the Incarnation. The meat which is "sanctified by the word of God" is no longer to be called unclean because the great Cleanser has Himself, in taking humanity upon Him, entered into close relations with all organic nature. Nor is there anything disturbing to reason or unwelcome to faith in such a conception of the wide issues involved in the fact that God became man. Some such conception seems to be forced upon us by science, if we view man with reference to his origin, as part of the material universe, rather than with reference to his destiny, as made in the divine likeness. It is a principle of Christian philosophy that the Incarnation has far larger relations than those in which we see ourselves to be directly concerned. That the lower

* As Hooker supposes. See *Eccl. Pol.*, II., iii. 1

forms of life cannot be excluded from the influence of this great cosmic fact, was a feature of early Christian teaching which perhaps we have suffered to remain too much in the background. But however true such a doctrine may be, it seems hardly possible that this is what St. Paul had in his mind when he spoke of food being "sanctified by the word of God and prayer." Such a conception, though perhaps not to be described as foreign to St. Paul's theology, does not appear to have occupied any large share of his thoughts. The word of God seems here to be the word written, rather than the Word Incarnate; it is the Scriptures of the Old Testament rather than Him to whose advent they pointed.

In the Gospels we have, as it seems, a more decisive instance of the same usage of the phrase whose meaning we are trying to determine. "Ye make," said our Lord to the Pharisees on a famous occasion, "the word of God of none effect through your tradition." * Certainly, at first sight, the meaning of this seems obvious, and little open to dispute. The fantastic learning of the Rabbis had so obscured the principles of the divine law that it was hardly available for practical guidance. The fence placed round the law was so elaborately constructed that, if it served on the one hand as a safeguard, it

* St. Mark vii. 9-13.

also proved to be an impassable barrier. The word of God had been made of none effect by reason of the traditions with which the ingenuity of commentators had hedged it about. And the Messiah, who came not to destroy but to fulfil the law, declared that these barriers must be swept away, that the law must no longer be kept in this unapproachable sanctuary, but brought out into the light of heaven that it might once more serve as a guide to the footsteps of men. The plain meaning of the Fifth Commandment was in danger of being forgotten because of the subtle casuistry by which methods of evading it were reduced to a system. The written law was losing its supreme place in the religious life of the Hebrews, and this because of the glosses, every day increasing in number, with which the sacred text was being overlaid. The word of God was being made of none effect through the traditions of those masters of Israel, whose privilege it was to act as its authorised interpreters. It is not too much to say that "the word of God" in this context seems most naturally to refer to the sacred books of the Jewish Canon. And it is not unimportant to observe that in the parallel account in St. Matthew's Gospel * of the episode under consideration, the same phrase, "the word of God," though

* St. Matt. xv. 1-9.

not to be found in our authorised version, is yet present in the best Greek texts.

To be sure, there is another alternative which the context does not exclude. If anyone chooses to say that here is no reference to any collection of canonical writings, but that the phrase λόγος θεοῦ is used as the equivalent of ἐντολή θεοῦ, that "the word of God" means simply the Fifth Commandment, which was being made of none effect by the Rabbis, it is not possible to prove to demonstration that he is wrong. Such an interpretation is at least admissible, and affords good sense, though it does not seem to give as much point and force to our Lord's rebuke as does the simpler and more usual explanation, which I have attempted to defend.

As the result, then, of this somewhat intricate inquiry, it seems that we are justified in asserting that in two passages at least of the New Testament, one from the Pastoral Epistles and one from the Synoptic Gospels, the phrase "the word of God" seems most naturally to point to the Old Testament Scriptures and to them alone, while beyond all controversy in a large number of other passages such a reference, though not involved in the context to the exclusion of all other meanings of the phrase, would have been admitted as legitimate by the apostolic writers.

As we pass onward from apostolic times we find indeed that the title which has been under discussion is but rarely applied to Holy Scripture in the early literature of the Christian Church. But the language of Origen is very remarkable and not to be overlooked. We must read the Scriptures with reverence, he tells us; for if we use great care in handling the Eucharistic elements, we should remember that it is no less an offence to disregard the word of God than to disregard His body.* Thus it would seem that the great Christian teacher of Alexandria regarded the title "God's word" as not only applicable to every expression of God's revealed will, but as applicable in a special manner to the sacred books of the Jewish and the Christian Church. And this is, to some extent, a confirmation of the opinion which has been adopted on other grounds, viz., that the phrase as understood in this sense is not foreign to the usage of the New Testament writers; for we can hardly suppose Origen to have introduced or sanctioned a new phraseology of so striking and signi-

---

* Hom. xiii. *in Exod.* p. 176. See also Hom. v. *in Jerem.* § 16. He interprets Heb. iv. 12 of Scripture in Hom. ii. *in Jerem.* § 2. The strict phrase "the word of God" as applied to Scripture is frequent by the time that we get to Chrysostom. Compare Augustine *in Ps.* cviii. 1 and cxxix. 1. The phrase has thus, at the least, good patristic authority.

ficant a character, without giving some intimation of its novelty.*

Mr. Ruskin, indeed, has assured us† that it is a grave heresy to declare a group of books accidentally associated to be the word of God. And, of course, to anyone who believes that the books of the Bible have come together by a kind of happy accident, and that no superintending Providence overruled the gradual formation of the Canon, such a use of language will seem, if not heretical, at least unwarranted. But the apostles and evangelists certainly did not regard the Old Testament as "a group of books accidentally associated," nor did the Christian teachers of the early centuries so regard the books of the New Testament. With St. Paul the early Church believed that Holy Scripture was written for the instruction of the faithful, that in it, though "in sundry portions and in divers manners," the divine message was delivered, and so believing she did not shrink from calling the Bible the word of God. What is involved in this phrase is a large question, which must be postponed to another occasion; for the present it is sufficient to have considered the evidence of its actual employment in primitive

* Cf. also *Bab. Sanhedrin* 99a, "He who says that Moses wrote even one verse [of the Pentateuch] of his own knowledge is a denier and despiser of the word of God."
† *Fors Clavigera*, xxxv., xxxvi.

Christian literature, both within and without the Canon.

And yet once again. When we are bidden to cast away this time-honoured phrase as likely to mislead, we must ask ourselves what is the extent of the demand made upon us. Are we merely asked to keep clear of it in our ordinary preaching, as cautious people avoid any turn of language as to the grammatical accuracy of which they are doubtful? We are asked a great deal more. We are asked, in effect, to dismember that book of Common Prayer which is, next to Holy Scripture, the most valued heritage of the Anglican communion. We need only turn over its familiar pages to remind ourselves how rooted is this phrase in the language of Christian devotion. Into every part of the reformed Prayer Book this title of Scripture was introduced by the compilers, and introduced in a context which unmistakably emphasized its meaning. In the Exhortation in the Mattin office, as in the office for Holy Communion, in the Order for the Visitation of the Sick, in Collects, in Litany, in the Ordinal, as well as in the Homilies set forth by authority, we find Scripture called the word of God, and presented to us as therefore affording the standards of Christian doctrine, the models of Christian life. Whether we desire it or not, it will be impossible to eliminate this expression from our religious phraseology without removing much that is most dear and most precious in our book of Common Prayer. And this consideration is sometimes altogether left out of account.

But whatever may be thought of these questions of interpretation, no man who believes in a supreme Providence watching over the best interests of mankind, and who believes that the education of the human race is ordered by a divine spirit, will dare to say that the wonderful literature enshrined in the Bible does not contain " words of God " to us, lessons of life as well as of doctrine, for our guidance in this world, and through this world to that which is to come. It is in this literature that He who is Himself the true Word of God is presented for our adoration. And it is His voice that says to us across the ages, " Take ye heed how ye hear."

THE WORD OF GOD.

"Thy word is a lamp unto my feet, and a light unto my path."—Ps. cxix. 105.

Preached before the University of Dublin,
Advent Sunday, 1893.

THE WORD OF GOD.

WE were considering last Sunday the usage of the New Testament writers as to the remarkable title, "The word of God," which so frequently occurs in Scripture, and is so common in our religious phraseology. It was observed that the phrase is used in one of two contrasted, though connected, senses, either as expressive of God's revealed message to the world whether spoken or written, or as descriptive of the person of Him in whom that revelation centres. And this usage of the New Testament writers has continued down to our own time. Since the earliest ages every branch of the Christian Church has applied the title to the written word and to the Incarnate Word alike.

Nothing at first sight could be more extraordinary than such a use of language. To speak of a person as the "Word" is hardly more curious than thus to speak of a collection of writings on religious topics, even though those writings be the flower of the literature of a race truly gifted, as has been well said, with a genius for religion. And if, as we saw is at least probable, such twofold application of the term λόγος is not an afterthought of the Christian consciousness, but can claim the sanction of apostolic practice, it becomes of considerable interest to determine in the first place what is the precise force of the title, and next to inquire whether help towards the solution of the difficult problems now agitating men's minds as to the character and authority of the word written may not be obtained by recalling the history of the somewhat similar controversies which convulsed Christendom in the early centuries as to the person of the Word Incarnate.

And, first, as to the meaning of the title. The purpose of all speech is to convey to others the ideas which we have in our minds; the *word* is the sensible sign of the inward *idea;* it is the idea itself brought into practical relations with human life. And it is thus not a mere random or inarticulate utterance; it is the expression of rational character, it is the manifestation of that reason in respect of which it is written that man was made in the divine image. It is only by such outward expression that ideas become realised in practice; for only in this fashion can they be communicated to mankind. The word is the outward expression of the rational idea. Ideas, it is obvious, acquire in this process definiteness and clearness of outline. They can be communicated, criticised, discussed. Were it not for some such external realisation, they would only appeal to him in whose mind they originated; they could not enter into the consciousness or guide the conduct of his fellows. But it is to be observed that if by means of such outward expression the idea gains in precision, it loses in content. The process of definition is also a process of limitation. In proportion as language is skilfully chosen, it excites in the hearer the counterpart of the idea which the speaker has in his mind; but the greater and more novel the idea, the more difficult is it for any words, however precise, to call it up in the consciousness of another. In the very act of expression something is lost. It is plain, *e.g.*, that this is true of the ideas of every poet who is anything more than a mere writer of verse. He may be never so great a master of form, and yet if he be really a great thinker as well, his language will not be competent to reproduce exactly his thought. In the very act of translating his ideas into words they are impoverished; as expressed in speech, they lack that completeness and breadth of range which we attribute to the inspirations of genius. And great poetry is great not only for what it says, but for what we feel is unsaid, for that spirit which underlies the letter, which influences us half unconsciously, a spirit which we find ourselves wholly unable to grasp or define. In short, the word, if it is the expression of the rational idea, also of necessity imposes limitations upon it. So much seems to be implied in the meaning of the term.

And thus, when we find St. John calling Him " the Word" who is Himself the supreme revelation of the Eternal, it seems to be quite consonant with this phraseology that St. Paul should say of the Son of God that, in becoming man for man's sake, "He emptied Himself,"* that He became voluntarily subject to those limitations which existence in this world on the plane of human life necessarily involves. God as the Word came into direct contact with humanity, and this contact itself, as it seems, involves a limitation, though the manner and degree of that limitation we may be quite incompetent to fix. And when we reflect on the fact that the same title came to be given in process of time not only to the Redeemer Himself, but to those Scriptures which heralded and recorded His advent, we feel that in this manner of speaking a profound lesson may be conveyed. The Scriptures are the word of God. Yes; but then we remember that, except,

* Phil. ii. 8.

perhaps, in the bare intellectual region of pure mathematics, words are never adequate to the corresponding ideas. There is always the necessary limitation consequent on definition. This is true of human speech; much more must it be true of a divine revelation, inasmuch as the thoughts of God infinitely transcend the thoughts of men. It is not only that men may not be able to appreciate or grasp the divine view of life and duty, but that in the very act of revelation there must be an accommodation to the conditions of the medium by which it is transmitted. The revelation may be—must be—as infinitely superior to its expression in human speech as that expression is superior to man's comprehension of it. Holy Scripture is the divine word, but it is spoken to men, and, therefore, according to the old saying of the Rabbis, it is spoken in the language of the children of men. The record of the revelation is subject to the limitations consequent upon the employment of human speech.*

But we may perhaps go somewhat further than this. It was observed by a remarkable English writer of the seventeenth century,† and his obser-

* Newman, *University Sermons*, xii., 264, has a fine passage on this subject.

† *I.e.*, J. Smith, in the first of his *Select Discourses on Prophecy*. The passage is quoted in Lee's *Inspiration of Holy Scripture*, p. 363, and the analogy is sharply criticised in the preface to the third edition of that book.

vation has now become almost a commonplace in Anglican theology, that the twofold employment of the title " the word " for the person and the message of the Son of God, suggests an instructive analogy between the Word Incarnate and the word written. As our Lord to some extent " emptied Himself," to use St. Paul's phrase, of His divine prerogatives in taking human flesh upon Him, as He became truly man in the act of incarnation, so does it appear that in the written word there are traces of human agency as well as of divine inspiration. As we recognise a union of two natures in the divine person of the Christ, we are not perplexed or surprised to find that there is again a mingling of the divine and the human in the Christian Bible. In applying the analogy, indeed, we must be careful not to overlook a fundamental difference between the two cases. Our Lord's human nature is without flaw; He is not only man, but perfect man; He is the perfect revelation of the divine will and purpose. We cannot make any such categorical statement about the human element in Scripture. The revelations delivered, as the apostolic writers tell us, to the fathers through the prophets were confessedly imperfect, progressive, changing; the revelation in Christ was perfect, final, eternal. In the one case we have to do with a permanent, in the other with a merely provisional, revelation of the divine counsels. But although the analogy is thus no more complete than analogies usually are, still it has for us a lesson not without value.

If we let our thoughts travel back to the history of the controversies of the fourth and fifth centuries as to the person of our blessed Lord, we shall perceive that the centre of the difficulty then lay in this very expression λόγος, or " Word," which is now perplexing the minds of Christian people when applied to Holy Scripture. It seems almost as if the controversial history of those centuries was repeating itself amid the changed circumstances of our time. Without losing ourselves in the labyrinths of subtle speculation in which so many lost themselves in former ages, we may see that the forms of error with which we have now to contend are merely old foes under new faces.

The strange doctrine of the heretical teacher, Apollinarius, which declared that our blessed Lord had no human soul, but that its place was taken by the divine reason, is not unlike a theory of Holy Scripture into which devout minds have often been drawn—the theory that there is really no human voice speaking to us in the books of the Bible, but that their authors were but the passive instruments of the Holy Spirit, far removed from the ordinary conditions of humanity. No one who has thought upon the matter will hesitate to say that it was with a true instinct that the Church of the fourth century rejected the effort of Apollinarius to place the Redeemer at so great a distance from His redeemed, as would deny Him a share in their intellectual nature; and it would be a like mutilation of the truth for us in the nineteenth century to deny that in the sacred pages of Scripture the strivings of human souls are really depicted for our learning.

Or to press the parallel a little further, as may be permitted in a University pulpit. What was the heresy of Eutyches, who refused to admit a distinct human nature in Christ, but an endeavour to raise the divine Saviour above the passions and humanity of men? Well meant, we need not hesitate to say; but does anyone regret the decision formulated by the Church at Chalcedon that this too was a perversion of the truth? That there is a human nature, no less than a divine, in the person of our blessed Lord, is not a mere barren dogma of speculative theology. It needs not argument to show that it affects, consciously or unconsciously, the very springs of our Christian life. For the Church to have sanctioned the denial of a true human nature to the incarnate Word would not only have impoverished Christian theology; it would have robbed the story of the Crucified of its matchless power over the lives of men.

And may not something of the same be said of Holy Scripture, the written word? We do not want, in practice, to remove the Bible from the plane of life; we want to emphasize its value for life. We dare not treat it like a sacred fetish;* what we desire above all is to appropriate to ourselves those lessons of faith and duty which were recorded for our instruction under divine guidance by men of like passions with ourselves.

Or once again. A view of Holy Scripture that seems to be gaining support at present is this, that while there is a recognition of the value of the message contained in "many parts and in divers fashions in that literature, it is supposed that we may pass by as of little moment large portions of its teaching as unsuited to the age. There is prevalent a tendency, openly avowed in some quarters, to say, This part of the Bible is inspired; that part is not. This was written for our learning; that has little of permanent value. The morality of Christ, for instance, we shall try to follow, as far at least as is socially convenient; but for the record of the actions of Jael

* Cf. Martensen, *Christian Dogmatics*, p. 403. He urges that although the phrase 'The Scripture is the Word of God' expresses the union of the human and divine in Scripture, we must not so insist on this union as to exclude any distinction.

(as well as for the actions themselves) we have nothing but reprobation. Not to speak of the confusion as to the meaning of the word *inspired*, which is involved in such statements, it seems worth observing that to distinguish sharply in this way the human and divine voices in Scripture, to mark off parts as recorded without divine supervision, while in others the hand of God is recognised, is really to make a mistake for which we have an exact parallel in the history of the doctrine of the Incarnate Word.

The very head and front of the offending of the heresiarch Nestorius was this, that he distinguished a human and a divine personality in the Word who was made flesh, that, perplexed by the problems of the Incarnation, he was bold to say that the man Christ Jesus was not the Son of God. What did the Church say to him at Ephesus ? We need not concern ourselves now with the methods by which this controversy was practically closed, for European minds at least; we are only concerned with the result, without regard to the policy by which it was brought about. And the declaration of the Church was that it was not consonant with the revelation with which she had been entrusted to place reliance on any such formula as that proposed by Nestorius; that it was impossible thus to find in Christ a human personality distinct from that of the Incarnate Son of God, and that the person of Jesus was indeed divine. It may be said that this is an obsolete controversy. Perhaps so; and yet it would be hard to find a closer parallel to the modern theory we are considering, as to the complex character of Holy Scripture, than is afforded by the Nestorian heresy. To both the answer is the same: What God hath joined together we dare not put asunder.

We do not live in the days of general councils, whatever may be the precise degree of authority which we may be inclined to attach to their decisions. But it is worth remembering, for our peace in days of intellectual distress, that the Church found her safety in early ages by refusing to commit herself to any theory as to the person of the Saviour. The problems which presented themselves for decision then were very like the problems which vex us now. What many minds among us seem to desire is a cut-and-dried formula expressing the union of divine and human in the written word. The Christian intelligence of the fifth century was sorely distressed because a similar formula could not be elaborated as to the Incarnate Word. The Church refused, on the one hand, to accept the theory of Apollinarius, or the still more subtle theory of Eutyches, which declared that our Lord's human nature was imperfect or unreal. Such a theory, she saw, would not fit the facts of the case; it was not in harmony with the record of the Gospels, even as it would not satisfy the soul seeking a Redeemer. And again, she refused, still more sternly, to listen to that "division of persons" which would have presented two strangely-united beings to our reverence instead of the eternal Son of Man. But she offered no counter formula for the acceptance of the faithful, for the decree of Chalcedon did no more than assert the fact of the union of the divine and human in the person of Christ without expressing any logically complete theory as to the mode of that union.

And thus the lesson which history has for us, in our present distress, is the need of patience and faith. We dare not be hasty. The conscience of modern Christendom, which with quickened intelligence and wider knowledge largely occupies the place formerly filled by the decisions of a general council, finds itself unable to adopt a theory as to Scripture so entirely at variance with the facts as that which would exclude the wills and the characters of men from the composition of that divine library which we have learnt to call the Bible. So far, well.

And, on the other hand, the Christian Church has as yet refused to sanction any such division of territory in the Bible as has been proposed by some speculators, both orthodox and unbelieving. She holds the voice of Scripture to be a divine voice, though it speaks through human, perhaps fallible, lips.

Again, so far well. But we have not penetrated to the root of the matter if we do not perceive that no formulæ can circumscribe the word of God, whether the Word Incarnate or the word written. A revelation, from its very nature, must be impossible to define with exactness. We must frankly recognise whatever traces of human imperfection may be found in the pages of Scripture, as we must be equally ready to recognise that divine Spirit which, it is not too much to say, gives something of an organic character to the general body of literature therein contained. Further than this we may never be able to go. It will probably never be possible to set forth with logical precision the conditions under which the divine voice speaks to the children of men.

It may be urged that this is but a poor and unsatisfactory result. And to those who demand positive pronouncements on all topics of religion and of life, it will seem no doubt unsatisfactory to be told that it is unsafe to lay down any theory as to the mode in which the divine and human elements are blended in the Bible. But it is better, as Augustine tells us, to hesitate about things hidden than to contend about things which are uncertain.* There is an

* "Melius est dubitare de rebus occultis quam litigare de incertis." (Aug. *de Gen. ad Litt.* viii. 5).

ancient maxim, said to be found in the pages of the Talmud, which gives us a wholesome warning: " Teach thy tongue to say, I do not know." If we are content to take the Bible as it is, honestly determined to accept the truth about it, whatsoever that may prove to be, we shall be bearing ourselves as faithful learners in the school of Christ.

As we go through life we learn more fully day by day that it is not the broad and easy path, whether of speculation or of practice, that is the path of safety. The Master to whom alone we look for counsel and guidance, tells us, even as He guides us, "Strait is the gate, narrow is the way."[*] Difficulties we must expect in the solution of every problem of revelation, ay, of every problem of life. But the presence of difficulties will not deter us, if we be wise men, from the path of duty. Indeed, if we did not come to the Hill Difficulty at some time in our journey we should begin to suspect that we had wandered from the road to the heavenly city. And the cry of the prophet comes to us this Advent season with a message of comfort and hope, as it bids us be of good cheer, for the day is coming when all that is now dark shall be illumined with the light of the divine Presence, when, even here on earth, " the crooked shall be made straight, and the rough places plain."

[*] St. Matt. vii. 14.

THE RESURRECTION OF THE BODY.

"But some man will say, How are the dead raised up, and with what body do they come? Thou fool, that which thou sowest is not quickened, except it die: and that which thou sowest, thou sowest not that body that shall be, but bare grain, it may chance of wheat, or of some other grain; but God giveth it a body as it hath pleased Him, and to every seed his own body."—1 Corinthians xv. 35—38.

Preached before the University of Dublin,
Second Sunday after Easter, 1892.

THE RESURRECTION OF THE BODY.

AMONG the many topics suggested by Eastertide, there is probably none of more intense personal interest than the subject of that future life to which every Christian looks forward as confirmed to hope by the resurrection of our blessed Lord. " I am," He tells us, " the Living One, and became dead, and behold I am living for evermore;"* and it is the constant theme of Scripture that the resurrection of mankind is morally consequent on His resurrection. " As in Adam all die, even so in Christ shall all be made alive."† The prospects of humanity are not bounded by the grave; they stretch out into an infinite future full of splendid possibility. So much, indeed, seems to be suggested by nature itself; for it is an almost universal instinct of mankind to believe that the grave is not the end, but the very gate of life.

* Rev. i. 18. † 1 Cor. xv. 22.

In proportion, however, to the strength of the conviction with which we hold this momentous belief, our curiosity becomes excited as to the nature of that undiscovered country to which we are hastening. We inevitably go on to ask questions as to the character of that future state of existence to which we look forward—questions which, for the most part, are impossible to answer with confidence. Reason can do little, except to assure us that, though we cannot fully understand the conditions of life in the invisible world, yet its happiness or unhappiness must very much depend on our manner of life here. The presages of conscience lead us to anticipate a righteous judgment at the world's assize, but they do not give us any insight into the way in which reward or punishment will be bestowed. And the hints given in Scripture are few and scattered; its teaching is rather negative than positive. The felicity of the blessed is not literally described; the pictures in the Apocalypse are but sketched in outline. In like manner the punishment of the wicked is spoken of with such indefiniteness, both as to its nature and its duration, that there has been fierce controversy within the limits of the Christian Church as to the final relation of the impenitent to the great Judge. Our Lord Himself seems to have spoken with singular reserve on this topic. When pressed by Sadducee cavillers with an old theological puzzle as to the future life of a person who had been married more than once, He dismisses the difficulty by reminding the objectors that nothing but confusion can possibly result from applying the conditions of earthly existence to the existence enjoyed in heaven. We have no right to expect natural law everywhere in the spiritual world.

But there is one point—and that the really important point—on which the witness of Scripture is express. The future life is one of continued *personal* existence; the same person who lives and works here will continue to live and work hereafter. Death is thus a mere episode in personal life; not its termination. The Christian heaven is not a state of unconscious life, like the Buddhist *Nirvana;* it is the sphere of those higher activities which are begun in this world. And the language of Christian devotion is full of this conception. In the Collect for to-day* we speak of the true knowledge of God being itself everlasting life, even as we pray in other collects that we may be granted here that knowledge of God's truth, which is in the world to come life eternal. The life of the future is begun here, and one side of its activity is expressed by that knowledge of God, which it is man's chief business on

* Collect for St. Philip and St. James's Day.

earth to attain. Now this continuity between the present and the future life of the Christian is brought into full, even startling, prominence in an article of the Christian creed, which we are too much accustomed to leave in the background. "I believe," we daily say, "in the resurrection of the body." Let us consider for a few moments some consequences of the belief expressed in these words.

Philosophers, it may be safely said, have never succeeded in explaining fully and clearly the mutual relations of the body and the soul of man; but it is matter of ordinary experience that the functions of the one are closely bound up with the functions of the other. We can see, perhaps, that conscious life is abstractly possible without the aid and co-operation of a bodily organism; but we can form no picture as to the manner in which the existence of a disembodied spirit could be manifested. We cannot represent to ourselves work, fellowship, affection, even knowledge, except through the instrumentality of an organism of some kind; and so as we believe that in the future all these and kindred activities will continue, we say that we believe in a resurrection of the body.* A disembodied spirit would be quite a different creature from the complex being

* See Liddon's *Elements of Religion*, Lect. iii. § iii.; and the Duke of Argyll's *Reign of Law*, p. 283.

man. So much, perhaps, we might reason out for ourselves without the aid of Scripture; but all reasonings about the unseen world and the state of the departed so easily glide into extravagance, that we gladly lay hold on the reassurance given by the Christian revelation, that the forecasts of reason were not mistaken on this point.

There are, of course, the gravest difficulties in the way of formulating our belief. St. Paul brings out one of the most serious, as well as one of the most obvious, of these in the text. "Some man will say, How are the dead raised?" Is it to be supposed that those identical material particles which we lay in the tomb are to be collected together again by a stupendous miracle at the last day; that the actual body laid in the earthly sepulchre is to be quickened hereafter for life eternal? Is the prophet's vision of the divine breath descending on the valley of dry bones to be taken as giving a literal picture of the scene of the general resurrection?

Now with reference to the physical anomalies involved in this theory, which are often brought forward as an objection to the doctrine of the resurrection, it must be observed that there is nothing in them impossible to faith for anyone who believes in the miraculous. God could, we need not hesitate to say, beyond all hope or thought, reproduce hereafter the same material body that has lived here on earth. And, moreover, the belief that He will do so derives some support from the fact of our Lord's resurrection as described in the Gospels. The Christian Church has always believed that the very body of Christ, which was laid in the rock-hewn tomb, was preserved from corruption, and raised again to a new and glorified life. "It is I myself," He said to His disciples after He was risen: "behold my hands and my feet; handle me and see; a spirit hath not flesh and bones as ye see me have."* And it might be supposed that, as this resurrection is the type of ours, as the resurrection of Christ is the potential resurrection of every son of Adam, our bodies will, in like manner, be reproduced on the day when the last trumpet shall summon every soul to judgment. But the truth is, that arguments from analogy of this kind are extremely precarious, and must be applied with great caution. From the nature of the case the body assumed by the Incarnate Word must have been quite peculiar in character; we know that He had a power over it which does not belong to men, and it cannot be contended that all the properties which it had can be transferred to our mortal frames. His body in the tomb "saw no corruption," and as in

* St. Luke xxiv. 39.

this particular the analogy between His death and ours breaks down, it cannot be urged that in all other respects it must be exact.

It would appear, then, on the whole, that although the doctrine of the resurrection of the body in its crudest and most literal sense must not be ruled inadmissible because of its miraculous character, although further it cannot be denied that the circumstances of our Lord's resurrection give it some plausibility, yet we dare not erect it in this sense into an article of faith. And, indeed, whatever may have been held on the subject by pious Christians in later times, the theory in question was certainly not held by St. Paul. The whole point of his answer to the caviller in the text rests on the principle that it is *not* the natural body that is to be raised, but a spiritual body which will be a fit organ and instrument for the redeemed soul. "If there is a natural body," he says, "there is also a spiritual body." "Flesh and blood cannot inherit the kingdom of God; neither doth corruption inherit incorruption." "Thou foolish one, that which thou sowest is *not* the body that shall be."

It is plain from St. Paul's language that he wishes to insist on the essential difference between the body that is laid in the tomb, and the body through which and by means of which the soul is to manifest its activity hereafter.* The one is subject to the laws of corruption and decay, fettered by the conditions of space and the ordinary laws of nature; the other, like the risen body of Christ, freed from those conditions and laws, transfigured as it were, but still not altogether out of relation to the body that was in earthly life the soul's companion. And the illustration that St. Paul uses to explain, as far as may be, this relationship between the earthly and the heavenly tabernacles, is full of significance. "That which thou sowest is not quickened, except it die; thou sowest not the body that shall be; but God giveth it a body even as it pleased Him, and to each seed a body of its own." And this seed is "sown in corruption and raised in incorruption; sown in dishonour and raised in glory." But yet "to each seed a body of its own," for "all flesh is not the same flesh." In the natural order the character of the crop depends upon the kind of seed that was sown. The corn in full ear has but little outward resemblance to the seed from which it has sprung; but if the latter be poor or of bad quality, so will be the former. And so the illustration of Scripture forces upon us the grave thought that the risen body bears upon itself the character of the earthly. In his own body is it true that "whatsoever a man soweth that shall he

* This is insisted on by Origen in his reply to Celsus, v. 18, 23.

also reap,"* both here and hereafter. The impress of character acquired here on earth follows the man, both in his body and in his spirit, into the world to which death ushers him.

There is another aspect in which there is much of hope and consolation to be drawn from this doctrine of Christianity, that the soul in the future will be conditioned by a body which, though glorified, yet bears traces of its earthly warfare. The Christian future is not one of lonely and self-sufficing felicity. We speak of it as a time of reunion, not of isolation, of undying affection, of fellowship with one another as with God. What makes death so terrible, so joyless, to those who look for no habitation eternal in the heavens is that it marks for them the end of friendship, of companionship, of love. Death thus cuts short human affections just when they have become so steadfast that they could not be changed by any other force in the world. And there is a natural shrinking from the unutterable loneliness and horror of an infinite future lived without those we love. This is not a mere sentiment; far from it. It appeals to the principle brought home to us every day more and more by science, that nothing in nature goes to waste; that the achievements of natural forces all point to something ever greater in the

* Gal. vi. 7.

future that lies beyond. But if death be the close of all earthly love, then we have arrived at this most irrational conclusion, that the greatest thing in the world is destined, after a few brief years, to pass away, or to survive but as a memory and a dream. No! if that be the natural destiny of human friendship and human affection, then is man enormously over-provided with altruistic instincts. Unlike other faculties and organs, his faculties of forming and keeping friendships and companionships are greater far than is needful or even desirable for the practical conduct of life.

The Christian doctrine of a resurrection of the body cannot, it may be granted, be demonstrated by pure logic; but, even apart from revelation, we can see that it satisfies the legitimate needs of reason, which demands that no faculty of man shall be wasted, even as it satisfies the cravings of the heart when it bids us sorrow not as men that have no hope: for the future life is not only a blissful state of spiritual existence, but is a life in which there may be glad recognitions, and a renewal and continuance of our nearest earthly companionships. When we say, "I believe in the resurrection of the body," we are really expressing our belief in a future in which intercourse and communion may be conceived as natural, even as necessary.

One further question St. Paul suggests: "With what body will they come?" I suppose the question has occurred to everyone who has thought upon a future life at all. How will those appear who have gone before us? The resurrection body, that is, the organism by which the spirit will manifest itself, will, we doubt not, in some way, though not necessarily in any way that we can now conceive, present sufficient points of resemblance to the earthly body to make identification possible. But a man's body here, his appearance, his character, change from day to day, from year to year. "With *what* body will he come?" Is it the body of youth, of manhood, or of old age? The approach of death often brings great changes in mental vigour, as in physical strength and beauty, before its actual arrival. Are we to suppose that those who have died will take up life again in the future with just that amount of intellectual power, of pious affection which they had been able to preserve up to the very moment of departure? It may be so, and yet there is something unsatisfying in such a picture. We have no certain information on the matter; but St. Paul, in one remarkable passage, seems to give a hint of another possibility. It has been thought by some* that he

* This is the view expounded in the *Summa Theologiæ*, Pars 3ª, *Quaest*. xlvi. art. ix. § 4. See also Martensen. *Christian Dogmatics*, p. 487.

alludes to the future life when he speaks of the Christian ideal being attained in that day when we shall all have come " to a perfect man, to the measure of the stature of the fulness of Christ."* If this be a legitimate interpretation to put on the words, then has St. Paul given an answer to the question, " With what body shall they come ? " The man will be perfected as far as his nature is capable of perfection. Our spiritual bodies shall all possess that state which corresponds, using the language of this world, to the perfect humanity in which Christ rose from the dead. For He, as the head of the human race, is the ideal of youth, of manhood, and of old age alike.

It will be said, I make no doubt of it, that these are the most extravagant of speculations, that they are based on no evidence worth listening to, and that it is simple waste of time and opportunity to speak on such topics. And in so far as it is meant that certain special conclusions which have been indicated are not *de fide* for any believing Christian, it is quite true; we are not given any accurate and detailed information as to the unseen world. But if it is meant—and this is sometimes meant by such objections—that the conditions of life in the future are too little known to be taken into account by prac-

* Eph. iv. 13.

tical persons who have their work to do in the world, then is it most untrue. The important thing for us is to do our work here, no doubt; but the way in which we do our work largely depends upon whether its consequences are believed to be permanent or only transitory. An unpractical subject! Why, it is the most practical of all subjects, for it deals with the eternal results of daily conduct. For him who can say with St. Paul, " death is swallowed up in victory," who has grasped the truth that love must always abide as well as faith and hope, because the Lord of life and love has triumphed over death; for him the music of Easter bells, which is still ringing in our ears, can bring no more practical or inspiriting counsel than that of St. Paul, "Be ye, therefore, steadfast, unmovable, always abounding in the work of the Lord, forasmuch as ye know that your labour is not in vain in the Lord."

THE UNITY OF THE SPIRIT.

"Endeavouring to keep the unity of the Spirit in the bond of peace. There is one body and one Spirit, even as ye are called in one hope of your calling : one Lord, one faith, one baptism, one God and Father of all, who is above all, and through all, and in you all."—Ephesians iv. 3—6.

Preached before the University of Dublin,
Whitsun Day, 1895.

THE UNITY OF THE SPIRIT.

THE grounds of St. Paul's exhortation to the Christian congregations of Asia Minor to be at unity and peace among themselves, were such, we may hardly doubt, as would have been recognised as convincing by any Christian of the first century. The apostle does not argue them at length; he states them with a simplicity which points to their universal acceptance. And, as is natural, we find that on the whole his reasons appeal to us as well as to those to whom they were originally addressed. That there is only one God and Father of us all is the first principle not only of Christianity, but of all the religions of the Western world. That there is only one baptism for the remission of sins is a confession which we make every time that we recite the Nicene Creed. That the members of the Christian society share in one common hope is a necessary consequence of their faith in one Lord. And such thoughts carry with them the reflection that those who are thus linked in holy bonds of faith and hope should give diligence to keep the unity of the spirit in the bond of peace.

But the duty of unity is urged by St. Paul on other grounds than these. He uses one illustration, in particular, which has not the force in the present condition of Christendom that it had in his day. There is, he says, "one body and one Spirit." He does not contemplate the possibility of any doubt or hesitation about this. He places it on the same level as his statement of the unity of the Godhead, and of the common faith and hope into which Christians are called by their one baptism. One body, as one spirit. The metaphor is impossible to mistake. In common speech the spirit is the source of the life of the animal body; it works, indeed, through a complex organization, but the life which pervades the whole is one. A body is maimed if it have lost some of its members; and, even if it be not thus crippled, it will be unfit to discharge its various duties if each organ does not co-operate with every other. There is no divided life, although there be many members. So, St. Paul teaches, does the Spirit of God, one and unchanging, display His power in and through a marvellous organization which is called the Body of Christ. And were it not that we have grown callous from familiarity, it would be startling to come upon such a picture of the unity of the Christian society, and thus to recognise how far removed is the reality from the ideal. But whatever we may think about it, St. Paul declares that the Christian Church is as truly one body, as that there is no division or plurality in the Spirit who is the giver of its life.

And so it is not unfitting that on Whitsun Day, the festival of the Spirit, we should be directed to turn our thoughts to the unity of that body of Christ which is quickened by the breath of the Spirit of God.

The subject, it will be said—it has been often said—is somewhat barren; for there are few projects less capable of speedy realisation than that of the re-union of Christendom. It is *impracticable*, men say; let us not waste precious time in thinking about it. And certainly the outlook is gloomy enough; he must be either very sanguine or very ignorant, or both, who thinks that the project is easy of accomplishment. On the one hand the Eastern Church regards itself as the sole depositary of the orthodox faith, and classes together Romanist and Protestant peoples, Latin and Teutonic races, as all alike heretical, though possibly in different degrees. On the other hand the Papal See lays claim to an exclusive infallibility, and declares with imperious voice that the only salve for the wounds of Christendom is to be found in acceptance of the Roman supremacy. And even those who cannot accept these extravagant claims are themselves not agreed as to the contents of the Gospel of Jesus Christ. The Churches of the Anglican communion and the countless religious bodies into which English-speaking peoples are divided are far indeed from exhibiting among themselves the unity of the Spirit in the bond of peace. The re-union of a divided Christendom! It is an idea so vast that it is hard to take it in. The effort to realise it—nay, the mere effort to pray for its accomplishment—requires large faith. The working towards it, in ever so poor a measure, will demand strong patience. It will not be accomplished in a year or in a century, if we may judge anything from the rate of progress in the history of the past. Our problem will be the problem of many generations yet unborn.

But is the problem, then, insoluble? Is the spectacle of a united Christian society never again to be seen on this earth? Is the effort to restore unity to the Church of Christ an effort destined to be in vain? Before we answer, let us recall a great historical achievement which Whitsuntide brings before us. We are so familiar with the existence of Christianity as a present fact, that we often forget at once its small beginnings and its extraordinary power of propagation. Possibly on the morning of the first day of Pentecost there may have been in Palestine a few hundred Christian believers, none, so far as we know, persons of any special distinction or position. The aim that these men set before themselves was truly audacious; it was nothing short of the evangelisation of the world. And what has been the result of their labours? Why this, that four hundred millions of human beings, one-fourth part of all the inhabitants of the earth, this day profess the name of Jesus Christ. The unity of the Christian society is sometimes spoken of as impracticable. Let us ask ourselves before we say so, Are the forces to be overcome really greater than those which beset the efforts of the early preachers of a Catholic religion proceeding from a despised Eastern province? We pray "Thy kingdom come," that is, we pray that the Church may be Catholic in fact as she is in name and in intention, that she may yet embrace "all sorts and conditions of men." And shall not the bountiful answer to that prayer inspire us to pray further, "Thy will be done" to Him who prayed "that they all may be one, that the world may believe that Thou didst send me"?* The unity of the Christian Church

* St. John xvii. 21.

is no more impracticable now than was its catholicity eighteen centuries ago, though in very deed for the fulfilment of the one ideal as of the other the breath of the divine Spirit must descend upon the world.

There are many things which seem impracticable when we do not really wish for them. It is easy to suggest imaginary difficulties; easy to magnify existing ones, provided that the will to overcome them be wanting. And so it is that the first step towards the achievement of the re-union of Christendom is to become conscious of the dangers we are in by our unhappy divisions, of the spiritual power which we lose by dividing our forces; it is to recognise that it is not the will of God that things should remain as they are. There have been times when no sense of the sin of disunion seems to have been present to Christendom. But indications are not wanting that there is a growing desire now in men's hearts to draw closer the bonds of fellowship between the various religious bodies which profess Christ as their Master. We may point not only to the utterances of individual piety, but to the authoritative declarations of those who speak on behalf of large sections of the Christian world. The conference held at Lambeth some seven years ago of all the bishops of the Anglican communion thought the subject one worthy to be pressed upon all the faithful. Nonconformist bodies have more than once expressed their desire that some basis for re-union might be agreed upon. It seems, to say the least, unlikely that immediate practical measures will result from the re-union conferences held yearly in Switzerland, but the fact that they are held at all shows the direction to which men's thoughts are turning. Or, again, the remarkable letter to the English people, recently issued by the Pope, however we may regret that there is no sign of willingness to modify the imperious claims of the Roman See, contains passage after passage in which every religious man will rejoice. And, finally, the friendliness of our relations with the Greek Church, and the interchange of courtesies between Anglican and Greek bishops in the East, indicate a temper which could not have been anticipated but a very few years ago. These various symptoms of Christian spirit are unmistakable; they afford ground for hope; the first step to re-union has been taken in the very effort to pray for it.

We shall be faithless if we call it impracticable; we give thanks for the growing desire for it. But there is sometimes a danger of forgetting that the unity of the body of Christ means a unity of faith as well as a unity of discipline. And we dare make no sacrifice of principle either on the one side or the other in our efforts to gain it. "Keep that which is entrusted to thee,"* said St. Paul to Timothy. The Catholic faith is a sacred *depositum* entrusted to the Christian society to guard and to transmit unimpaired. It is not an agglomerate of isolated and independent articles of belief, but an organic whole, impossible to add to, impossible to divide. Our plain duty is to make ourselves acquainted with it in its integrity, and to study with anxious care the interpretations of it put forward by those who are not of our communion. Thus only can mutual understanding be reached. Differences of principle can only be readjusted by unprejudiced study, personal and prolonged, of the cardinal verities of the faith, and after the fullest recognition that they are differences of *principle*. To ask our Dissenting brethren to sacrifice their principles before they have been persuaded that they are mistaken principles, is as unreasonable and, I will add, as irreligious as it would be to sacrifice our own.

For instance, it is sometimes said that there are really no important doctrinal differences between members of the Church of Ireland and members of the Presbyterian or Methodist bodies. Could anything be said more offensive or more insulting? For what it means, when analyzed, is this, that our non-

* 1 Tim. vi. 20.

episcopal brethren hold aloof from what is, at the least, the great historic Church of the country, and (outside the Roman Catholic body) the greatest force for spiritual life in the land, for no serious reason at all, that they thus wilfully perpetuate schism and disunion. How can anyone dare to say so who considers the gravity and learning and piety of many in these alien communions? No, we shall not promote reunion by alleging that there are really no obstacles to it. What is probably the greatest obstacle to union between us and Dissenters is that they understand us as little as we understand them; the obstacle is ignorance of the history of the past and of the conditions of the present. I plead, then, to begin with, that we may set ourselves to learn what our differences are, and then nothing but good can arise from sober and temperate discussion. To understand a problem is to have gone a long way towards its solution.

Once more, it cannot be too carefully remembered that sacrifice of principle will, in the end, postpone that very hope of unity which is the prayer of Christendom to-day. Premature remedies often aggravate the evils they are meant to cure. To sacrifice (as I pray God we in this Church of Ireland may never do) the conception of a historical society, living a sacramental life, for the sake of attracting our Dissenting neighbours, would, in so far, render the possibility of union with the Greek Church in the East, or with the Latin Church in the West, more and more remote. And no amalgamation can be a reunion of Christendom which does not include its largest section, nor would it be the unity for which our Lord prayed. True it is that the temper of the Roman Church is not conciliatory, nor is its system attractive to those who, like ourselves, come into daily contact with it; but yet to leave it out of consideration altogether in our hopes and our prayers for the future, is to betray that we have not realised at all what the unity of Christendom means.

I have said that no hasty sacrifice of principle will solve our problem. Are no sacrifices, then, needed? Yea, truly, many and great. Perhaps the hardest of all sacrifices is the sacrifice of prejudice. The struggle of the Christian Church towards catholicity, that struggle which is not yet accomplished, has not been carried on without the discipline of pain. The missionary enterprise of the Christian Society has not been fulfilled without the martyrdoms in life and in death of her bravest and her best. And it is not plain why we should expect that the establishment of her unity should be an easy matter, attainable with ease or without painful

effort. Nay, it will mean sacrifice, sacrifice of much
that we prize, and rightly prize; it may mean loss,
serious and disheartening. Is it not high time for us
to bethink ourselves what are the non-essentials, the
ἀδιάφορα, which we may be prepared to give up or
to accept if so be that we may gain some? Is it too
much to ask others that they too should consider
what they can abandon or what they can receive
without dishonour? It is hazardous to go into particulars, for in truth the determination of the essentials cannot be left to the caprice of individuals, but
is for the authoritative deliberations of the various
religious bodies affected. And yet some things there
are, especially those which relate to the conduct of
public worship, which we should do well, as a beginning at least, to recognise as of no great importance. The use of ceremonial, of symbolism, the
colour or the shape of an ecclesiastical vestment—is
it worth our while to dispute about these things,
whether on the one side or the other, for less or for
more, while men are disputing all around us whether
there be such a thing as sin, any need or possibility
of salvation? I do not say that it would be an easy
matter to give up our habitual practice in respect of
any of these; it might involve a real sacrifice. But
who can fail to see that it is not the abandonment or
the adoption of them that is the important matter,

but the recognition that they are as nothing compared with the essentials of the Christian faith?

And, indeed, we cannot hope with much confidence for union with other Christian bodies until we are first at one among ourselves. For this, at least, we may work. It is worse than mockery to speak of union among the various Christian bodies so long as we cannot recognise sincerity and piety in those who differ from us in our own. My brethren, if the lesson of tolerance is ever to be learnt by the Church of Ireland, the beginnings of that lesson must be learnt in this place. Where else shall it come from if not from here? Is it not the very office of a University to teach men to view things in their true proportions, to form a right judgment as to their relative importance? How save by education can that appalling ignorance be cured which seems not to recognise Christianity beyond the borders of our own prejudice or of our own narrow experience? There are few lessons a man learns at the University of more consequence to himself, be he cleric or layman, than the lesson that men may differ on all topics, political, social, and religious, and yet may be all honest and Christian men. If we do not apply it to life, if we dare to suggest dishonest motive wherever opinions clash with our own, we have miserably failed to learn our lesson. The message of Pentecost is a message to us that Christ is not always preached in the same language, that the voices of the Spirit are many, that He speaks by the mouth of every faithful servant of the One Incarnate Lord.

And yet education, by itself, is not sufficient to give this large and catholic tolerance, to inspire that charity which beareth all things, which hopeth all things. To be filled with that spirit we need to come into the divine Presence itself. Not in controversy but in worship shall we best learn to know and do the will of the Master who has willed that all men shall be one in Him. So shall we stretch out glad hands of welcome to the dawn, far distant, perhaps, as reckoned by human measures of time, but certain in the prescience of Him with whom a thousand years are but as one day—to the dawn of that Sun of Righteousness who shall come with healing in His wings. So are we content to say, in patience and in faith, " We wait for Thy lovingkindness, O God, in the midst of Thy temple."

THE ATHANASIAN CREED.

"He that believeth and is baptized shall be saved; but he that disbelieveth shall be condemned."—[St. Mark xvi. 16.]

Preached before the University of Dublin,
Trinity Sunday, 1895.

THE ATHANASIAN CREED.

BEFORE the revision of the Irish book of Common Prayer, a rubric prefixed to the Athanasian Creed directed its recitation on certain festivals of the Church, of which Trinity Sunday was one. And inasmuch as there is often some misapprehension as to the present claims of that creed upon the allegiance of Irish churchmen, it may be not altogether unprofitable to discuss its position in our formularies, and more generally its position and authority as a statement of belief in the cardinal doctrines of Christianity.

I do not propose to enter here into any of the large literary and historical questions which are involved in the determination of its date and authorship. The Thirty nine Articles, indeed, call it "Athanasius' Creed" without qualification; but no one is likely to claim infallibility for the Articles in a matter of this sort, and it is a universally admitted fact that, however it came into being, the symbol *Quicunque Vult*, as a Latin and not a Greek confession of faith, has no claim whatever to the authority carried by the name of Athanasius. Again, it has long been matter of dispute whether the document is or is not composite, made up of two distinct declarations of doctrine, drawn up possibly at different times, one on the subject of the blessed Trinity, the other on the subject of the Incarnation. The evidence has not yet been thoroughly sifted; but, so far as it has been made accessible, it does not seem to justify such a divorce between the beginning and end of the creed. But, however that may be, the origin of the symbol is wrapped in obscurity; we can say little more about it than that it is to be sought in Western Europe, not earlier than the fifth century.

It has, then, neither the antiquity nor the authority of either the Apostles' Creed or the Creed of Nicaea, and cannot be placed on a level with these, one of which is the confession required from candidates for baptism, the other from recipients of Holy Communion. Nor in use has it occupied the position of either of these venerable declarations of doctrine. It is customary to speak of it as a hymn or canticle rather than as a creed, and there is a certain plausibility in such a description. If we take up any ld Latin psalter, at the end we shall find an appendix of fifteen hymns, the *Te Deum*, the *Benedictus*, the *Magnificat*, the "Song of Moses" in Deuteronomy, and so on; and among these the hymn *Quicunque Vult* has a place. Moreover, until the revision of the English Prayer Book in the reign of Charles II., it was directed to be sung on certain days after the *Benedictus*, without, as it seems, any displacement of the Apostles' Creed at all. It was used as a canticle, to which its semi-metrical form lends itself, rather than as a creed proper; and its public recitation has often been defended on these grounds. But the truth is, in such an argument one important consideration is ignored. The collections of hymns in which the *Quicunque* is found were not originally made for the use of the laity; they were intended for the use of the monks and the clergy in the choir. The *Quicunque* was largely used, as has been said, in the Middle Ages as a canticle, but it formed no proper part of the devotions of the people. Thus, in the Sarum Breviary it was appointed to be sung at Prime, but this was hardly a service for laymen; and in some ancient canons in like manner its study by the clergy is enjoined, but no mention is made of the laity. The use of antiquity, therefore, whatever weight attaches to it, is distinctly against the recitation of the Athanasian Creed by the people in public worship. And inasmuch as it is not altogether easy to understand, a good deal of it being quite unintelligible without some little knowledge of ecclesiastical history, we may be satisfied with the wisdom of the course taken at revision, when the rubric directing its public recitation was expunged. It was originally a rule of faith, not a hymn; and even when it came to be used as a hymn, it was not at services in which those unskilled in theological phraseology took any large part.

But the fitness of the *Quicunque* for liturgical use is one thing; its value as a definition of the faith is quite another thing. And it is not well to forget that, for the clergy at least, subscription to the Athanasian Creed stands exactly on the same footing that it did before revision. We still retain the Eighth Article, in which it is declared that "The three Creeds . . . ought thoroughly to be received and believed; for they may be proved by most certain warrants of Holy Scripture." Whatever binding force the Thirty-nine Articles have, the Athanasian Creed has the same. Nay, more, in the new preface to the Irish Prayer Book, written in 1877, the statement is deliberately made: "With reference to the Athanasian Creed (commonly so called) we have removed the Rubric directing its use on certain days; but, in so doing, this Church has not withdrawn its witness, as expressed in the Articles of Religion and here again renewed, to the truth of the Articles of the Christian faith therein contained." It is desirable to bear this in mind, for people sometimes speak of the Athanasian Creed as "rejected" by the Church of Ireland, when it really occupies exactly the same position as a rule of faith that it has done since the Reformation. It is to be received with the same loyalty that the Thirty-nine Articles claim, and it may be interpreted with whatever degree of freedom is regarded as legitimate in their case.

And, indeed, the parallel case of the Articles helps us a good deal. They furnish convenient standards of doctrine, expressed in language which, as originally meant to meet certain emergencies of the day, in some instances bears traces of having been somewhat hastily chosen. They are not the articles of the Christian faith in which every person to be baptized professes belief; these are to be found in the Apostles' Creed. Nor are they even required to be accepted by every faithful member of the Church, as is the Nicene Creed. Their office is to furnish standards of doctrine for those who have to teach; and they are, as is natural, drawn up in language that cannot be appreciated without some acquaintance with the controversies of the Reformation period. And the like may be said of the so-called Athanasian Creed. It is an exposition of doctrine on the subjects of the Holy Trinity and the Incarnation, expressed in almost every verse in language which has reference to some error once prevailing on these great topics. We sometimes hear disparaging language used about certain clauses which seem to us unmeaning; but we forget that the very fact of the disappearance of the heresies aimed at, is in large measure due to the use of the Creed itself. Sabellianism, Monarchianism, Macedonianism; they are, perhaps, little more than names now, at least in Western Christendom, but their extinction has been largely assisted by the defining standards of the *Quicunque Vult*.

It is, however, notoriously a fact that difficulties are felt about subscription to the *Quicunque*, which are not felt in relation to the Thirty-nine Articles; and it is time to consider these more in detail.

First, then, as to the clear cut and dogmatic character of its declarations on such mysterious questions as the nature of the Godhead and the conditions of the Incarnation. It is plain, to begin with, that our acceptance of them depends largely upon *ex animo* acceptance of the Christian revelation. Do we or do we not believe that a revelation was made to the world in the person of our Lord Jesus Christ on these great matters? If not, *cadit quæstio;* the Athanasian Creed is so much theological lumber, but the Nicene and Apostles' Creeds must go as well. But if a revelation has been made, embodied in the New Testament, and entrusted to the Christian society to transmit, we need not be surprised if more is contained in the *credenda* of the Church than is matter of fair deduction from the elementary principles of natural religion. It is sufficient if they contain nothing which contradicts those principles. Now, the first half of the Athanasian Creed is nothing more than an amplification, with much variety of statement, of the theses that God is a personal Being, and that this divine Personality is not single and isolated, but triple and with inner distinctions. That personality may be predicated of the Supreme is indeed a proposition to which reason itself might lead us, inasmuch as personality is the highest category of thought. And it is suggested in that earliest page of revelation, where we read that man, personal being as he is, was made in the image and likeness of God. Further, the best thought of the world about God, even before Jesus Christ came upon earth, everywhere tended to recognise that this highest personality must contain in itself the possibility of relations. There must have been, men have said to themselves, outlets for the love of the Supreme even before the creation of man or of the world. And thus the teaching of Christianity in reference to this sublime topic added emphasis and authority, as well as distinctness, to the beliefs to which devout souls had been led by reverent contemplation of their Maker. But how is all this to be expressed in language which can be understood by the masses of mankind? I do not know how else save by some such collection of clauses as those which follow the statement that "There is one Person of the Father, another of the Son, another of the Holy Spirit. But of the Father and the Son and the Holy Spirit, the Divinity is one, the Glory equal, the Majesty co-eternal." The *Quicunque* is not a philosopher's Creed; far from it. It was intended to guard simple men from distortion of the doctrine they had received. It is the very negation of metaphysics, the refusal to tolerate their intrusion into the circle of revealed truth.* But for all that, it would be agreed by Christian theologians of all schools that its definitions on the subject of the Holy Trinity and the Incarnation, though in the former case at least somewhat crudely expressed, are fair deductions from the revelation of the New Testament.

By Christian theologians, I said; and this leads us to a second remark. The *Quicunque Vult* has no reference in its intention or in its language

* Cf. Mozley's *Lectures and other Theological Papers*, p. 189.

to those who are outside the pale of the Christian Church, to those who have never heard of Jesus Christ or have been imperfectly instructed concerning Him. Its opening sentence, which speaks of *holding* the faith, holding that which has been already received, might teach us as much. Neither here nor elsewhere, however, can we trust the ordinary English rendering, which is really only a translation of a translation. The printing of a Greek copy at Basle, together with the traditional authorship of the great Bishop of Alexandria, led the Reformers to think that Greek, not Latin, was the original language of the Athanasian Creed. Thus they translated from the Greek copy before them, and so arose our Prayer-book version, which, as reaching us in this way through a double translation, is far from an accurate representation of this ancient Rule of Faith. What does it actually say? " Quicunque vult salvus esse, ante omnia opus est ut teneat Catholicam fidem." " Whosoever wishes to be safe, to be in that state of salvation of which the Catechism speaks, as the normal condition of members of Christ's Church, must hold the faith of that Church; and that faith must be kept whole and uncorrupted." That is not a very difficult matter to agree to. If the Church of Jesus Christ be indeed the ark in which men may ride safely through the waves of this troublesome world, I do not know what less can be said than that to those who know the truth, to whom the faith of Jesus Christ has been presented in its integrity, disloyalty to known truth, abandonment of faith, is perilous. And so the Creed goes on: "The Catholic Faith is this, that we worship one God in Trinity and Trinity in Unity." "Who, therefore, wishes to be safe, let him thus think," not "he *must* think," but "let him thus think of the Trinity." "This is the Catholic Faith which except a man believe with fidelity and firmness, he cannot be safe." So all through; it is the safety which is guaranteed within the pale of the Christian society, not the condition of those who have no share in its graces, that is the main object of contemplation.

But, it will be said, you have avoided all the harsh expressions in the Creed which grate upon our ears. What is to be said about the so-called damnatory clauses? Is it not a dreadful thing, it is asked, to pronounce such sentence upon those who, perhaps through no fault of their own, through involuntary ignorance, or through some peculiarity of mental constitution, find themselves unable to assent to all these complicated formulæ? "Which faith," for this is the sentence especially disliked, "except a man keep whole and undefiled, without doubt he shall perish everlastingly." It is hardly necessary to say that no new dogma is introduced by these clauses into the belief of the Christian society as to the future condition of the faithless. The precise connotation of the word αἰώνιος, "eternal," in the Gospels, may be fair matter for discussion. It is a matter upon which there is serious difference of opinion among good scholars, among faithful sons of the Church. But all that is relevant to our present purpose is to observe that it means no more and no less in the Creed than it means in such phrases as "everlasting fire," "everlasting punishment," which were used in a like reference by our merciful Lord Himself. This is not any private opinion; and it may be a relief to some minds to hear again the deliberate and wise pronouncement of the Canterbury Convocation of 1879 with reference to these clauses: "The warnings in this Confession of Faith," it was said, "are to be understood no otherwise than the like warnings of Holy Scripture; for we must receive God's threatenings, even as His promises, in such wise as they are generally set forth in Holy Writ. Moreover, the Church doth not herein pronounce judgment on any particular person or persons, God alone being the judge of all."

The truth is, that the objections to these clauses do not really derive their persuasiveness from any speculative difficulties attending their reception, but from the fact that they appeal with power to a certain habit of mind, a certain mental disposition. I mean that disposition which is averse to the contemplation of anything unpleasant, whether in religious or in secular matters. It is so much more delightful to dwell on the promises than on the warnings of the Gospel that men shrink from the revelations of the wrath of the Lamb. There is, for instance, a temper which refuses to submit to the Commination Service on Ash Wednesday, and puts forward as the reason that we ought not to judge our neighbours. Such criticism is as shallow as it is popular. In neither Athanasian Creed nor Commination Service is any use of the optative mood. The sentences of the divine judgment are declaratory; they are not threatenings of ours, but warnings of God. No one would venture to contend that those who are deliberately guilty of the sins solemnly enumerated on Ash Wednesday are anything else but accursed in the sight of the All Holy. And, seeing that men are accountable for their faith as well as for their practice, will any one venture to contend that, speaking in general terms, eternal safety in this world and the next may be confidently looked for by those who reject the faith of Jesus Christ when it is offered to them? If any so think, they have greater and more solemn words than those of the Athanasian Creed to reckon with. " He that believeth and is baptized shall be saved ; but he that disbelieveth shall be condemned."

And, lastly, lest any one may think that the Creed lays more stress than is equitable on right belief as distinguished from right conduct, consider, I pray you, its end. When all is said about faithful and firm belief, what is the sum? Is it not this? "They that have done"—not they that have believed, or thought, or said anything, but— "they that have done good shall go into life everlasting, and they that have done evil into everlasting fire." A mediæval superstition, do you say? Nay! it is the voice of Scripture, it is the voice of conscience, it is the voice of God.

THE CHARACTER OF ST. THOMAS.

"And Thomas answered and said unto Him, My Lord and my God."—St. John xx. 28.

Preached at an Ordination held in St. Patrick's Church, Ballymena, by the Lord Bishop of Down and Connor and Dromore, St. Thomas' Day, 1890.

THE CHARACTER OF ST. THOMAS.

IN the character of St. Thomas, upon which the Church invites us to meditate to-day, there seem to be certain features of peculiar interest to the men and women of our time. Little, indeed, is told about him in the Gospels; he comes into prominence on three or four occasions only; but yet we are enabled from these slight and fragmentary records to obtain as complete a picture of his personality as is possible in the case of any other of our Lord's companions. One reason, doubtless, which may be assigned for the vivid impression produced by the anecdotes of his life which have come down to us, is the fact that he seems to have been a man ever ready to run into extremes. No cautious, safe, sober disciple was St. Thomas; there was nothing in him of the comfortable self-contentment of modern Christendom. That spirit of indifference which we sometimes mistake for a broad and catholic tolerance was foreign to his whole nature; his impetuosity arrests our attention from its unlikeness to the popular religion of our own day.

This feature in his character is conspicuous in the first notice of him that we find in the Gospel according to St. John. When our Lord told His disciples of His intention to go to Bethany, because Lazarus was sick, they tried to dissuade Him. "Master," they said, "the Jews of late sought to stone Thee; and goest Thou thither again?"* But there was one among that company who would not hear of his Master facing any danger in which he had not a share. "Then said Thomas unto his fellow disciples, Let us also go that we may die with Him." He is ready to follow Christ even to death. As we see from the record of his feebleness a few weeks later, his perception of the superhuman dignity of Christ's person was not by any means so clear as that of his associates; but he was second to none in the warmth of his love. He was not one of those who cautiously weigh the rival claims of Christ and of self; he despised calculation of consequence, and was eager to be loyal, at all cost. So is it often still. As long as the cross which lies in our path is only one of labour or of self-denial, we think we would be ready to take it

* St. John xi. 8.

up. It is a spirit with which many, brought up in Christian homes, begin the Christian life. Many a child on the day of its confirmation has felt something of this spirit of devotion. The Master has bid us follow Him; we will follow Him, we are sure, to the end. A happy, a blessed, thing, never to lose that first enthusiasm of simple faith; but yet is it not true that the reason why St. Thomas's history touches many hearts in our own generation, is that they have felt that faith in danger of slipping away from them, as it did from him?

For, as it turned out, the devotion of the apostle, though it could brave death, was not proof against the assaults of doubt. The stages of the mental process he went through are plainly told. On the night of the Last Supper, when our Lord comforted His friends, distressed at the prospect of His approaching death, by promising them His speedy return, and by holding out to them bright hopes of a joyful future in the heavenly mansions, it is St. Thomas who interrupts that mysterious discourse with the question: "Lord, we know not whither Thou goest, and how can we know the way?"* That question is significant of the man's temper; he desires to *know*, rather than to *believe*. So far, as long as the mysteries of faith have not been presented to him, he has been quite

* St. John xiv. 5.

untroubled; he has felt no difficulty in his allegiance. He loves his Master and that is enough for him. But now, when he sees that there are many things in religion he does not understand, when He finds that in the Master's own discourses are many "hard sayings," his natural impetuosity forces him to speak. He cannot remain silent as if he acquiesced, when indeed he does not. He must ask for fuller light. "Lord, we know not whither Thou goest, and how can we know the way?" That one may see the way without having the final goal in view is not intelligible to him. He has been accustomed to think everything in religion so easy; he does not understand why the beatific vision is not vouchsafed to him even here and now; he cannot brook the idea of mysteries of faith. And so he goes on, in all honesty as it would seem, until his doubt culminates in the denial of his Lord's resurrection: "Except I shall see in His hands the print of the nails, and put my finger into the print of the nails, I will not believe."* That is to say, knowledge is to precede faith. In his first unthinking stage he assumed that his faith was genuine knowledge; it seemed so simple. But when his eyes are opened, when Christ shows him that there are many things he cannot expect to comprehend, his devotion re-

* St. John xx. 25.

ceives a shock. Has his love, then, been resting on a phantom of the imagination? He will not, in any case, be again deceived. He will no more walk by faith, but by sight. And he finds at last, by bitter experience, that such a principle involves the abandonment of Christ.

Here is the very course of modern unbelief marked out. The demand for complete knowledge has been made by many since the days of St. Thomas. To be content to follow Christ in life's journey without having the promised land in clear view, is regarded as childish. To accept mystery as a necessary element in a revelation from God to man, is thought superstitious. But we shall see the root of this dreadful mistake if we ponder on the words in which St. Thomas made his confession of faith when the Saviour came again into his presence. "My Lord and my God," he said. Here was the solvent of all his difficulty and the explanation of all his doubts. The Teacher whom he had followed, who had deigned to associate with him in closest fellowship, was not only a loving Master; He was Himself the Almighty God. He had expected to find no mystery in the teaching of Christ because he did not see that there was any exceptional mystery in the person of Christ. But it is now revealed to him by the divine mercy that the Lord of whose resurrection he had doubted was in truth the One whose death was the real marvel. That the Prince of Life should not be confined by the grave was, indeed, fitting and congruous to the nature of His claims. That there should be much that is mysterious in the words of Christ will cease to offend us if we remember that the whole advent of Christ from the Conception to the Cross was a mystery, than which nothing can be more inexplicable. The Word who became flesh is a mystery, but yet a mystery which explains all else. Once this central truth had been accepted by St. Thomas everything else became plain. His faith was no longer the unstable belief of sentiment; it was a conviction, for which his whole nature, his reason as well as his heart, was responsible. It satisfied alike his deepest intellectual cravings and his heart's dearest hopes. "My Lord and my God." No greater confession of faith than this is recorded in the Gospels. No apostle grasped with more firmness the divine miracle of the Incarnation than the once-doubtful St. Thomas. It was the rationalist among the apostolic company who was the first to put into plain language the truth they all felt, the truth of the Godhead of our Lord Jesus Christ. It was a thought, very possibly, from the expression of which they had recoiled; they had put it from themselves. But St. Thomas, not satisfied until he had gone to the very root of the matter, sees that here alone is the answer to his doubts, the justification of his preaching, the source of his hope.

My brethren, who to-day seek holy orders, in the life of this doubting apostle there is for us something for imitation, if there is much, also, from which we pray to be kept free. We pray to be kept from the weakness which beset him; and shame on us if we were not stronger than he, with aids to faith so manifold in which he could not share! But there is something, too, of a noble example in St. Thomas. He was, as we have seen, a man of extremes; no half-measures pleased him. He would die for Christ, if need be, though his faith was not as strong as his love. But even in his weakest moments one virtue shines out, his absolute honesty. He would not profess anything he did not feel. There are few dangers to which one who has constantly to do with sacred truths is more exposed than that of letting himself say more than he has warrant for in his own personal experience. At certain crises there are certain things a clergyman is expected to say; it may be a crisis of religious controversy, it may be a crisis in the life of his humblest parishioner. Whatever it be, if he dares to say more than he knows in his inmost heart he is justified in saying, he is false to that truth with which he is intrusted. Nothing is so dangerous, nothing so disloyal to Christ, as unreality. It does no good, for it always unmasks itself in the end; but a far more serious thing is that it is in the highest degree dishonouring to the Gospel. I do not speak of conscious deceit—God forbid!—but rather of that tendency to exaggerate the truth, to which we are all so liable, with the intention of giving force and point to what we have to say. If the priest be true to his charge he will keep a watch over the door of his lips, and never say anything to his people to which there is not something of response in his own heart. St. Thomas's history, sad though his fall was, may teach us the blessing that attends honesty. The Lord did not reject His unworthy servant; He made plain to him His truth. And so through that doubting apostle was the fact of the Resurrection made more certain for us. It was, as we say in the Collect, "for the greater confirmation of the faith" that St. Thomas was permitted to be doubtful of the Lord's resurrection. Here, indeed, is a lesson of encouragement, if also of warning. Out of our very failures, if we be but true, the Church of Christ will be the more built up and edified. It is in weakness that strength is made perfect.

But, again, the story of St. Thomas gives to us, to whose office it belongs to feed the Church of God, a lesson in *method*. We begin at the wrong end if we begin with anything short of the doctrine of our Lord's incarnation. It was because St. Thomas had not put into words this central fact of faith, and faced its consequences, that he came so near to falling away from grace. It is just because we do not always put it in the forefront of our teaching that men's difficulties as to minor points become so magnified that they seem destructive of Christianity. If the Church of Christ is to be saved from that barren Deism which is ever reappearing under new forms, we must look to it that the truth of the Incarnation is taught by us fully and plainly. Not that men deny it openly: no, indeed! but, like St. Thomas, they have never faced it; they do not see what it involves. That God became man; that He who was born in a manger and suffered on the cross for man's redemption was not only God's messenger, but God Himself; that the Carpenter of Nazareth, the Prophet of Galilee, was the Christ, the Son of God: what a light this throws upon all that we teach! It makes all the difference whether or not we thus habitually think of our blessed Lord. It will materially affect all our beliefs as to His Church, His sacraments, His ministers. A society set up on earth for men's edification by Jesus the Son of Mary—that would be one thing; a Church founded and guided by Almighty God—that is a very different thing.

Pledges of the Saviour's affection, signs of our loving remembrance—these would be good things; sacraments instituted and blessed by the Word who was made flesh—these are, indeed, better things. Men set apart for human convenience that the Gospel may be duly preached—that is one way of looking at the office of the Christian minister. But how different will be our conception of the dignity of that office, if we remember that the words which will presently be said to those who this day seek the order of priesthood were first used by One who had power in Himself to bestow the greatest of gifts. "Receive ye the Holy Ghost," said the Lord to His Church; and He who gave that solemn benediction is "the same yesterday, to-day and for ever." Be sure that we imperil the stability of the whole system of Christian doctrine if we misplace its centre of gravity. That centre is the fact of the Incarnation stated with absolute simplicity in the confession of the apostle, "My Lord and my God." We can teach nothing greater; we dare teach nothing less.

Here is our common message; here, also, is our common strength. We are members of a kingdom that cannot be shaken, for it is not in our own strength that we are equipped for our mission. We hope to preach the " word of truth "; it must be in the "power of God."* Our hearts may well leap at the thought that whatever other men's trade or business may be, ours is to try to teach the world the truth as God has revealed it to His Church in the person of His Son. But who are we that we should undertake such a responsibility, if we had not a hope that He who gives us the desire to begin this work will also give us power to fulfil it? It is beyond man's capacity; our strength must come from Him who is our Lord and our God. But as partakers in that common humanity which He has for ever ennobled by joining it to Himself, as sharers in that common redemption which He has wrought for the children of men, as members of that universal Church to which He has promised His perpetual presence, we may hope for strength. And as we pray that the sevenfold gift of the Spirit may be poured out on those who to-day gird on their armour, and prepare to fight as leaders in the army of Christ, He will surely listen. He will surely give us His blessing that so we may increase and go forwards from strength to strength.

* 2 Cor. vi. 7.

THE GRACE OF ORDERS.

"Unto every one of us is given grace, according to the measure of the gift of Christ."—Ephesians iv. 7.

Preached at an Ordination held in Christ Church Cathedral by the Lord Archbishop of Dublin, Third Sunday after Epiphany, 1892.

THE GRACE OF ORDERS.

ST. PAUL brings before us in these words a great principle, underlying, as it would seem, the general method by which God's spiritual gifts are distributed among men. He tells us that grace is given to all Christians; but that, although this be so, it is not given in the same degree and fashion to each: " unto every one of us is given grace," but it is given " according to the measure of the gift of Christ."

God's gifts are variously bestowed; He spake " in sundry portions and in divers manners "* by His servants the prophets; He gives to each nation, each man, that which is requisite for present needs, and that which will best serve the highest interests. Without doubt, all men are subject to the divine influence; no race, no condition, is excluded from the sunshine of a heavenly Father's love; He makes His sun to rise on the evil and on the good, and His spiritual gifts, we may well believe, are showered upon the world with the same wealth of liberality. But, never-

* Heb. i. 1.

theless, we can see for ourselves—and we are also frequently reminded in Scripture—that though He has never left Himself without a witness among men, yet the divine education of mankind is carried on through the instrumentality of favoured races or favoured individuals, to whom special gifts have been given for service.

The most familiar, and perhaps the most conspicuous, example of this in history, is afforded by the case of the Hebrew people. To them, as we believe, a clearer and more definite revelation of God's will was vouchsafed from time to time than was granted to other nations of antiquity. They were, emphatically, the chosen race. Grace was given to them, as far as we may judge, in greater fulness than to others. Their history was providentially overruled; their literature grew up under the care of the divine Spirit; their national hopes and aspirations were directed to the coming of a Redeemer who should consummate in Himself their national offices of prophet, priest, and king. And on a superficial reading of their wonderful history we might be inclined to feel a great difficulty on the score of justice, when we contemplate their position described in Scripture as that of "the peculiar people of God."*
They were *elected*, as we say, to a position of spiri-

* 1 Peter ii. 9.

tual privilege. What, then, are we to think of the position of those other great nations, the Egyptians, the Greeks, the Romans, who had to feel after God as best they might without the aid of any of those special warnings and revelations which the Hebrews were granted in such abundance? Is it that they were not so important in the sight of God? We cannot think so. Why, then, this seeming inequality of favour?

But the difficulty arising out of this apparently unequal distribution of spiritual gifts becomes very small when we ask ourselves the simple question: What was the object of this election or selection of the Jews? Was it that they should have a monopoly of God's highest gifts, a monopoly of the knowledge of His will and His grace? Not so—though many of them vainly so believed—but rather that by their means the whole earth should be "filled with the knowledge of the Lord as the waters cover the sea."* In short, the whole history of Israel is an object-lesson on a large scale which may teach us the method by which God reveals Himself to the world. The revelation is made through the fittest man, the fittest race; but it is for all. The literature of the Jewish race was "written for our learning" as well as for theirs. The hymn-book of the Jewish temple

* Isaiah xi. 9.

is still used in our Christian worship. Our Master and Lord, the Saviour of the world, was born of Jewish race. We shall not think that the Jews were unduly favoured when we remember that it is from Palestine that our whole western civilisation derives its religion; Japhet is dwelling in the spiritual "tabernacles of Shem."*

We are taught, then, from this history that although God's gifts are not given equally to all men, although they are given with more apparent generosity to one man, to one community, to one race, than to another, it is always in order that the divine education of mankind at large may be the better carried on, that God's kingdom may come more speedily. This concentration of grace is in order that it may be of the more catholic benefit.

And thus we may see that there is nothing unreasonable in the claim of the Christian Church that she is the recipient of special grace not given to those outside her fold. She does not deny —she never has denied—the many gifts bestowed by God upon those who are not yet incorporated into the body of Christ; she dares not deny the presence in them of many graces manifested by their fruits; but still she emphatically claims the possession of certain privileges which have been entrusted to her

* Gen. ix. 27.

keeping, as the oracles of God were to the Jewish Church—not, indeed, for her own peculiar benefit, but for the salvation of the world. She is not merely an organization devised by human agency for promoting spiritual life; she is not merely an association with a religious object; she is the home of grace. Of this she has, to be sure, no monopoly; God gives grace to all who diligently seek Him; but she believes that fuller measures of grace and more varied privileges may be found within her borders than can be found without. Viewed in this aspect the question sometimes asked: "Can I be saved without the Church?" will seem to be an entirely mistaken one. The real question for us is: "As Almighty God has established a Church, and as He has granted special graces to those within her fold, am I going to refuse or neglect them?" To take a somewhat similar case. Many of us believe—we cannot help believing —that the heathen who have never heard of the Saviour, may, if they live up to the light they have, be saved hereafter through the Saviour's world-wide mercy. But that does not at all excuse us from hastening to spread the Gospel among them. Our special gifts are given to us for the benefit of all; we hold our spiritual inheritance in trust, not as an exclusive property.

Consider, again, how this principle which we have

been considering, that God gives special graces under special conditions over and above the ordinary bounty of His providence, is exemplified inside the Church herself.

What is meant by the phrase "the grace of sacraments"? Surely it is not that no grace is given to men except through sacraments; surely we all believe that there are other means of grace, prayer, meditation, the reading of Holy Scripture and the like. But what is meant is, that in these divinely-appointed mysteries a grace is given to the human soul which is guaranteed under no other conditions. And so for us to say that we will not be over-anxious (suppose) about the baptism of our children or about frequenting the Lord's table, because grace is attainable in other ways, is simply to say that we wilfully reject a special blessing which is ready for us if we will but come in faith and ask for it.

Or again, we miss the true meaning of an ordination service, if we do not believe that God will give, in answer to the devout prayers of His Church, special grace to those who in obedience to His call are going forth in His name. There is indeed always something solemn and impressive in the undertaking of new duties and new responsibilities, even in a secular office. And there is a peculiar impressiveness in an ordination service, which brings before us the historic continuity of the Christian Church in a way in which no other service does—as we recall how services like this in all essentials have been held for eighteen hundred years, one generation handing on the torch of the Gospel light to the next. But an ordination is something more than the continuance of a splendid tradition. This office and ministry, as we shall be presently reminded, are not of man's devising; but were divinely "appointed for the salvation of mankind." The words of the service for the Ordering of Priests were, we may be sure, not chosen at haphazard; and they convey in the most solemn and deliberate manner that there is such a thing as the grace of orders. We are directed to pray that the sevenfold gift of the Spirit be poured out upon our brethren in the faith; and we believe that He who can give "all good gifts to them that ask Him"* will not refuse to hear our prayers.

It is true, indeed, that all Christian men and women may, and do, exercise priestly functions; the priesthood of all believers is abundantly taught in Holy Scripture. All of us, laity and clergy alike, may plead for those whom we love, and with whom we have to do, the merits of the one sacrifice for the sins of the whole world offered by the Incarnate Son of God. The unfortunate phrase which describes

* St. Matt. vii. 11.

the taking of holy orders as "going into the Church," has done much to obscure this great truth; it has led men to reason as if all Christians were not members of the Church and inheritors of its blessed privileges. "Ye are," says St. Peter, addressing the whole company of believers, "a royal priesthood." *

But yet there is a difference in order between the faithful priest and the faithful layman. To the former is entrusted a gift which the latter has not, a gift described by St. Paul as "the spirit of power, of love, and of discipline." † And this being so, we may see the meaning of the phrase used in the rubric to the ordination offices, where the preacher is directed to point out to the congregation "how necessary these orders are in the Church of Christ." We need not go so far as to say with Luther that, "if a man teach uncalled, it will not be without injury to himself and to his hearers; for Christ will not be with him." ‡ But yet though many of us would hesitate to adopt these words of the great reformer, it is plain that it is not a matter of indifference whether a man is duly ordained to this office and ministry, or whether he takes it on himself without being appointed thereto. If there is a special grace promised by our Lord to those commissioned by His Church to preach apostolic truth in accordance with apostolic order, it cannot be of little moment whether we avail

* 1 Peter ii. 9. † 2 Tim. i. 7. ‡ In Gal. i. 1, *tom.* v. p. 215.

ourselves of such a benefit or neglect it. And, precisely as in the other cases which we have been considering, this claim of a special *charisma* or heavenly benediction for the Christian priest, is not in any way inconsistent with our thankful recognition of the graces which God showers upon us all. "Unto every one of us is given grace," but it is given " according to the measure of the gift of Christ "—to each of us in our several stations and in our several capacities.

My brethren who this day seek holy orders, I make no doubt but that you feel the need of such gifts, such grace in the high office to which you aspire. It is a need that you will feel more and more day by day, as you come more into contact with human souls, and learn by experience how perilous a responsibility you have taken on yourselves. You may not—it is a sad confession, none of us do—respond fully to the grace offered you at ordination; but yet is it a gift which no man can take from you. And the possession of it constitutes your sole claim to act as the ambassador of Christ, and to speak with authority in His name. Not indeed that it will act of itself, as it were mechanically, without prayerful thought and anxious care. When our Lord spoke of His hearers as "the salt of the earth," in the same breath He warned them that "the salt may lose its savour."* "Neglect not then," said St. Paul to

* St. Matt. v. 13.

Timothy, but "be ever kindling up again the gift of God, which is in thee by the imposition of our hands." *

When St. Paul thus compares the grace of ordination to a fire or light, he suggests by his choice of words that it is a light which may easily be extinguished, and which needs constant tendance. It must be continually kindled into a flame if it is to shine forth brightly as a beacon in the darkness. So is it with all earthly light; it is ultimately derived from the light of the sun, but it will not shine out with a steady and brilliant glow unless care be taken that it is fed and nourished.

Once again, this comparison of the grace of orders to a light, suggests to us the purpose for which it is conferred. A lamp is of no service unless it illuminate the surrounding darkness; it has no worth in itself, except in so far as it fulfils this function. And so, too, the dignity attaching to the office of the Christian minister is of little avail, unless he be to the best of his poor ability a light to show men the way to God. " Ye are," said our Lord in the Sermon on the Mount, " the light of the world." †
That is the position assigned to all Christian men, and not least to the Christian minister in the economy of the Incarnation. God is the ultimate source of all light, as of all life; but if we keep our faces

* 1 Tim. iv 14; 2 Tim. i. 6. † St. Matt. v. 14.

steadfastly turned to Him, it cannot be but that some few rays of His light will be reflected from us. Such at least is our privilege; how far we fall short of it is known only to Him to whom all hearts are open and from whom no secrets are hid.

Thus the very essence of the office of the Christian priest is embodied in one word, *service*. If grace is given to us, it is not only for ourselves but for the benefit of others. If Almighty God casts His bright beams of light upon His Church, it is that they may be reflected into the darkest parts of the earth. And this is an aspect of the truth we cannot afford to overlook. Among the many peculiar temptations to which a clergyman is liable, there is none, I suppose, more subtle than the tendency to overestimate his own spiritual importance. It is so hard to impress upon others the dignity of our office, and at the same time to preserve our own humility of temper, that it is well for us to remember that the very purpose of the grace that confers dignity upon our office is that we may be worthy servants of the Church of Christ. " The sum of our labours," says Hooker, " is to honour God and to serve men"; and the object of all ministerial work on behalf of our lay brethren is, as set forth in the solemn words of the ordination service, that " they may be saved through Christ for ever." The less we think about ourselves and the more we think about our work, the better not only for our own spiritual advancement, but the better for our success in our vocation. But if, in thankful faith, we pray for the grace offered to Christ's ministers; if with honesty and singlemindedness we try to do our work as God has appointed it to us—not depreciating our office for the sake of popular favour, nor unduly exalting ourselves through motives of personal ambition—be sure that the sevenfold gift of the Spirit will not have been invoked in vain. "Unto every one of us" will be "given grace, according to the measure of the gift of Christ."

And lastly, what is the guerdon of faithful service for which we look? Is it that we may gain the approval of men? No. Is it that we may rest after toil with a satisfying consciousness of good work achieved? No. Is it that we may receive hereafter the crown set apart by the King for His loyal servants? It is this; but it is more than this. The true reward of service—for which we look with the more eagerness as we become more faithful in our ministry—is something that is not for ourselves at all. The end of our labour is service; and the crown of rejoicing of the true ministers of Christ is given to them when they hear the answer of His people to their invitation to "Come unto Him"—when their longing cry, *Sursum corda*, "Lift up your hearts," meets with the glad response, "We lift them up, lift them up unto the Lord."

The Gospel and the Age Series.

3/6 Large Crown 8vo, gilt top. **3/6**
EACH.   EACH.

1. **THE GOSPEL AND THE AGE.** Sermons on Special Occasions. By the late W. C. MAGEE, D.D., Archbishop of York.

SPECTATOR :—
"*Will arrest the attention of the world.*"

SATURDAY REVIEW :—
"*It is impossible not to be indebted to a champion who can defend the truth with such intellectual force and such choice incisive language.*"

RECORD :—
"*It contains the 'Gospel,' and it preaches to the 'age.' There is in all these sermons the excellence of a giant's strength.*"

CHURCH BELLS :—
"*The language is pure, clear, nervous, appropriate, energetic.*"

METHODIST TIMES :—
"*Beyond doubt one of the few volumes of sermons worth keeping in constant use as a spiritual and intellectual stimulant.*"

DUBLIN EXPRESS :—
"*They must be read and re-read in order that their originality of thought, strength of phrase, and noble orderliness of arrangement may be appreciated.*"

The Gospel and the Age Series.

3/6 Large Crown 8vo, gilt top. **3/6**
EACH.   EACH.

2. **GROWTH IN GRACE.** And other Sermons. By the late W. C. MAGEE, D.D., Archbishop of York. With an Introduction by His Grace the Archbishop of Canterbury.

GUARDIAN :—
 "*The sermons in this volume show us the Archbishop at his very best.*"

RECORD :—
 "*A fit memorial of a preacher of rare eloquence, who did not misuse his magnificent gifts.*"

CHURCH BELLS :—
 "*Through every line of them gleams manliness and power.*"

DAILY CHRONICLE :—
 "*Pervaded by the remarkable strength and spirituality of the preacher's mind, and addressed with striking force to immediate and practical ends.*"

LITERARY WORLD :—
 "*For eloquence and power of sustained thought, these sermons will take rank among the finest pulpit utterances of the day. We can unhesitatingly commend this volume as a great quickener at once of thought and of spiritual life.*"

The Gospel and the Age Series.

3/6 Large Crown 8vo, gilt top. **3/6**
EACH. ——————— EACH.

3. **CHRIST THE LIGHT OF ALL SCRIPTURE.**
And other Sermons. By the late W. C. MAGEE, D.D., Archbishop of York.

LITERARY CHURCHMAN:—
"*We give to this volume an unusually earnest recommendation, especially to the clergy. Such sermons as these are invaluable.*"

REVIEW OF THE CHURCHES:—
"*The book is full of a strong, vigorous, and masterful personality. There is much massive thought clearly expressed, much profound and significant reasoning, and an abundance of epigram.*"

GLOBE:—
"*It is hardly necessary to recommend discourses so full of fresh thought and vigorous reflection.*"

LITERARY WORLD:—
"*Marked by the strength of conviction and the eloquent force of language that characterised the author.*"

SCOTSMAN:—
"*The reader will find the generally accepted truths of Christianity set forth with a passionate earnestness, a wealth of illustration, and a power of argument and expression which cannot fail to command his attention and enchain his interest.*"

The Gospel and the Age Series.

3/6 Large Crown 8vo, gilt top. **3/6**

EACH. EACH.

4. **THE INDWELLING CHRIST.** And other Sermons. By the late HENRY ALLON, D.D., Minister of Union Chapel, Islington.

DAILY TELEGRAPH :—
  "*Worthy to take their place among the masterpieces of the old divines . . . . an enduring testimony to the greatness of a departed preacher.*"

CHRISTIAN WORLD :—
  "*A book which altogether is worthy to be called a great religious testimony.*"

BRITISH WEEKLY :—
  "*The final fruits of matured and ripened powers.*"

LEEDS MERCURY :—
  "*We are thankful that Dr. Allon's strong and tender ministry will still continue in this wise and helpful book.*"

SUNDAY SCHOOL CHRONICLE :—
  "*Altogether this volume will enhance Dr. Allon's reputation as a great teacher and great spiritual guide.*"

INDEPENDENT :—
  "*Word and thought are equally characteristic, and together mirror the ripe culture of the preacher's latest years.*"

The Gospel and the Age Series.

3/6 Large Crown 8vo, gilt top. **3/6**
EACH. ———— EACH.

5. **CHRIST AND SOCIETY.** And other Sermons. By DONALD MACLEOD, D.D., one of H.M. Chaplains.

SCOTSMAN :—
"*Admirable and seasonable discourses.*"

ROCK :—
"*Will do much to advance the consideration of great social questions on right lines.*"

GLASGOW HERALD :—
"*Very remarkable sermons they are.*"

RECORD :—
"*Fitted to supply a want of the age.*"

DUNDEE COURIER :—
"*Reverent without being conventional, and eloquent without being unrestrained.*"

EXPOSITORY TIMES :—
"*Though the treatment is designedly popular, there is plenty of first-hand knowledge displayed. There is also plenty of enthusiasm, plenty of courage, and plenty of assurance.*"

METHODIST TIMES :—
"*Business men will do well to add this volume to their library.*"

The Gospel and the Age Series.

3/6 Large Crown 8vo, gilt top. **3/6**
EACH.   ———   EACH.

6. **THE CHRISTIAN CERTAINTIES.** Discourses in Exposition and Defence of the Christian Faith. By JOHN CLIFFORD, M.A., D.D.

QUIVER :—

> "*Eloquent and incisive as these teachings are, they come as a valuable addition to the armoury of those who are fighting for the faith in an age when all men are asking first and foremost for certainty.*"

STAR :—

> "*On the ethical and social aspects of religion Dr. Clifford speaks with great freshness and impressiveness.*"

CHRISTIAN WORLD :—

> "*This book contains some of the brightest utterances on vital religious questions in the range of English contemporary theology.*"

WESTMINSTER REVIEW :—

> "*Vigorous and eloquent.*"

PALL MALL GAZETTE :—

> "*The book is a suggestive one, and will be read with keen interest.*"

The Gospel and the Age Series.

3/6 Large Crown 8vo, gilt top. **3/6**
EACH. ──────── EACH.

7. **CHRIST AND ECONOMICS.** In the Light of the Sermon on the Mount. By the Very Rev. C. W. STUBBS, D.D., Dean of Ely.

ECONOMICAL REVIEW :—

"*Plain, sensible, manly Christian teaching on the duties of citizenship, the evils of vulgar luxury, the proper use of wealth, and kindred topics. It is truly refreshing to find that there lives so faithful and worthy a disciple of Maurice and Kingsley—both in theology and social teaching.*"

INQUIRER :—

"*Full of the social teachings which the age most requires . . . . interesting and instructive from beginning to end.*"

ECHO :—

"*Full of the Christianity of Christ.*"

LEEDS MERCURY :—

"*The book is thought-compelling, and the stamp of broad but uncompromising patriotism is upon its eloquent pages.*"

CHRISTIAN LEADER :—

"*Full of knowledge, of courage, and of hope.*"

The Gospel and the Age Series.

3/6 EACH.   Large Crown 8vo, gilt top.   **3/6** EACH.

8. **CHRIST AND OUR TIMES.** By the Ven. W. MacDonald Sinclair, D.D., Archdeacon of London, Canon of St. Paul's, Chaplain to H.M. the Queen.

ROCK :—
"*We hope that these valuable discourses, which must have already, as spoken, been a blessing to many, may now, in their more permanent form of print, become a cherished possession in thousands of English homes.*"

SPEAKER :—
"*A brave and opportune book, which grapples in an honest and open fashion with many of the spiritual difficulties and social problems of the age.*"

QUARTERLY REVIEW :—
"*Very able and interesting sermons.*"

PALL MALL GAZETTE :—
"*Many of the questions which agitate or interest men's minds are discussed soberly and effectively in language studiedly calm and unimpassioned, but in words which will satisfy and even charm many a restless inquirer.*"

SUNDAY SCHOOL CHRONICLE :—
"*Very admirable sermons.*"

The Gospel and the Age Series.

3/6 Large Crown 8vo, gilt top. **3/6**
EACH. ——— EACH.

9. **THE LORD'S PRAYER.** Sermons preached in Westminster Abbey. By the Very Rev. F. W. FARRAR, D.D., Dean of Canterbury.

RECORD:—
  "*Intensely practical. . . . . They call with no uncertain voice to the careless and the impenitent; they touch the everyday life of the hearers.*"

REVIEW OF THE CHURCHES:—
  "*The Lord's Prayer has rarely, if ever, received so thorough and sympathetic an exposition, so scholarly and yet so practical. For the preacher this is, in our opinion, the first book on the subject.*"

EXPOSITORY TIMES:—
  "*These sermons are less an exposition than an illustration of the Lord's Prayer. And it is an illustration we are most in need of—an illustration as pointed, and rich, and fertile as this.*"

DUNDEE COURIER:—
  "*Their wealth of spiritual insight, their calm and exhaustive analysis, their simplicity, their literary finish, will make them to be prized by all.*"

SUNDAY SCHOOL TIMES:—
  "*Sure of a wide reading.*"

The Gospel and the Age Series.

3/6 Large Crown 8vo, gilt top. **3/6**
EACH.   EACH.

10. **THE COMRADE-CHRIST.** And other Sermons. By the Rev. W. J. DAWSON, Author of "Makers of Modern English," &c.

SCOTSMAN :—
"*All display originality of thought, simplicity of style, and vigour of treatment; the volume is sure of a welcome.*"

EXPOSITORY TIMES :—
"*Mr. Dawson's fertility in rapid, telling phrase — phrase that tells upon the ears of hurrying passers-by — is matchless.*"

MANCHESTER GUARDIAN :—
"*There is a real freshness and force of thought which lifts these sermons above the level of the conventional.*"

METHODIST TIMES :—
"*Fresh and poetic in conception, vigorous in utterance, and ever up-to-date; living sermons for a living age.*"

GREAT THOUGHTS :—
"*They deserve a place in every library. His words are winged, and full of life and energy. Vigorous, incisive, trenchant, they are often, as Julius Hare said of Luther's—'half-battles.'*"

CHRISTIAN WORLD :—
"*Fully maintains the high level of pulpit work shown in his previously published discourses.*"

The Gospel and the Age Series.

3/6 Large Crown 8vo, gilt top. **3/6**
EACH.   EACH.

11. **CHRIST AND SCEPTICISM.** And other Sermons. By the Rev. S. A. ALEXANDER, M.A., Reader of the Temple Church, London.

RECORD:—
"*Valuable contributions to the available defences of Christianity along its moral, historical, rational, and spiritual lines.*"

QUIVER:—
"*So high and strong in tone that all who are labouring in the field of Christian evidences owe to its author a deep debt of gratitude.*"

MANCHESTER GUARDIAN:—
"*Clear in style, and, without parade, show wide reading, and a mind thoughtful and earnest.*"

CHRISTIAN WORLD:—
"*An admirable volume of virile addresses.*"

SCOTSMAN:—
"*The book, which shows large acquaintance with the subject discussed, and is written in a calm, judicial, and sympathetic spirit, may be commended to religious inquirers who are repelled by narrow-minded dogmatism.*"

The Gospel and the Age Series.

3/6 Large Crown 8vo, gilt top. **3/6**
EACH.   EACH.

12. **LABOUR AND SORROW.** Sermons on various occasions. By the Rev. W. J. KNOX LITTLE, M.A., Canon of Worcester Cathedral.

CHURCH REVIEW :—
"This striking and powerful book contains within its pages much Christian philosophy, powerful rhetoric, and deeply emotional writing."

GREAT THOUGHTS :—
"A volume of brilliant sermons."

ECCLESIASTICAL GAZETTE :—
"We think this volume equal to any that has come from the writer's pen, and we wish it a wide circulation."

INQUIRER :—
"In these Sermons there is a precious mine of reading for every devout man and woman."

LONDON QUARTERLY REVIEW :—
"Suggestive and helpful, the outcome of much study of human nature, and God's ways of perfecting it."

The Gospel and the Age Series.

3/6 EACH.   Large Crown 8vo, gilt top.   **3/6** EACH.

13. **ESSENTIAL CHRISTIANITY.** A Series of Explanatory Sermons. By the Rev. HUGH PRICE HUGHES, M.A.

THE NEW AGE:—
 "*Preachers who wish to speak a living message to living men will do well to possess and ponder this vigorous volume.*"

PRESBYTERIAN:—
 "*The ground it covers, and the freshness of thought which pervades it, will be found to make it both instructive and stimulating to every Christian preacher and teacher.*"

SCOTSMAN:—
 "*Mr. Hughes puts life and originality into his sermons.*"

SUNDAY SCHOOL CHRONICLE:—
 "*An excellent book to put into the hands of young men who may be in danger of being drawn away into the dreary regions of unbelief.*"

LONDON QUARTERLY REVIEW:—
 "*Full of ardent evangelical zeal.*"

The Gospel and the Age Series.

3/6 EACH.   Large Crown 8vo, gilt top.   **3/6** EACH.

14. **VOICES AND SILENCES.** By the Very Rev. H. D. M. SPENCE, D.D., Dean of Gloucester.

GUARDIAN :—

"*A preacher who really studies such a volume as this will find that he has added very much to the solid matter which must provide the backbone of every sermon.*"

ROCK :—

"*The book covers pretty well the entire range of Church work, and is one which every one who takes up will read with pleasure.*"

MANCHESTER GUARDIAN :—

"*Earnest and interesting.*"

REVIEW OF THE CHURCHES :—

"*It has many excellent qualities — is devout, touched with emotion, and full of the most passionate loyalty to Christ.*"

METHODIST TIMES :—

"*Its practical homilies have a message for the times.*"

The Gospel and the Age Series.

3/6 Large Crown 8vo, gilt top. **3/6**
EACH.   EACH.

15. **TEN-MINUTE SERMONS.** By the Rev. W. ROBERTSON NICOLL, M.A., LL.D., Editor of "The Expositor's Bible," &c.

CHRISTIAN WORLD:—
"*A book to be commended to all Christian people. A book for weary spirits, for distracted and unsettled minds, for hearts world-worn and sorrow-laden, of every calling and sphere in life.*"

GLASGOW HERALD:—
"*Each one of them is a thoughtful, polished essay, as lofty in tone as it is straightforward and vigorous in expression.*"

INDEPENDENT:—
"*What strikes us very much in these brief sermons is the union of intellectual power with deep spiritual feeling.*"

LITERARY WORLD:—
"*It is a beautiful book, strong because so calm, suggestive, and only not eloquent because no room is found in it for mere rhetoric.*"

LONDON QUARTERLY:—
"*It will profit busy men who have leisure enough to digest as well as to read; and it will set preachers thinking.*"

The Gospel Series.

3/6 EACH. Large Crown 8vo, gilt top.

New Volumes.

16. **TEMPTATION AND TOIL.** By the Rev. HAY M. H. AITKEN, M.A., Author of "Love of the Father," &c.

17. **THE TEACHING OF JESUS.** By HORTON, M.A., D.D., Author of "R— and the Bible," &c.

18. **THE KNOWLEDGE OF GOD.** And Sermons. By J. H. BERNARD, D.D., of Trinity College, Dublin.

Other Volumes in Preparation.

ISBISTER & CO., LIMITED,
COVENT GARDEN, LONDON, W.C.

www.ingramcontent.com/pod-product-compliance
Lightning Source LLC
Chambersburg PA
CBHW022108230426
43672CB00008B/1318